IPHONE 15 PRO GUIDE

CW00434449

A Complete Step By Step Instruction Manual for Beginners & Seniors to Learn How to Use the New iPhone 15 Pro Max With iOS Tips and Tricks

BY

HERBERT A. CLARK

Table of Contents

Page |

Page |

Page |

INTRODUCTION

Announced at Apple's Wonderlust event, the iPhone 15 Pro Max is Apple's most Advanced phone ever. The new iPhone 15 Pro Max comes with a 6.7" OLED screen, a better camera, a faster chip, and more.

The device is available in Natural Titanium, Black, Blue, & White colour options

FEATURES OF IPHONE 15 PRO MAX

Design

The iPhone 15 Pro Max has basically the same design as the iPhone 14 Pro Max, but with more streamlined edges that change the feel of the phone in the hand.

Instead of stainless steel, the iPhone 15 Pro Max has a titanium band covering the front & back glass. Titanium is lighter than stainless steel, so newer models are lighter and the material is more resistant to scratches & dents.

The iPhone 15 Pro Max is 159.9mm tall, 76.7mm wide, 8.250mm thick, and weighs about 221g.

The pill-shaped Dynamic Island continues to sit at the upper part of the display, housing the True-Depth camera. The screen bezels have been significantly reduced this year for more screen space.

There's a power button on the right side of the device and an Action button & volume buttons on the left side. The Action button can be set to perform one of different activities; from activating shortcuts to turning on the flashlight, and it can be customized.

Under the iPhone, you'll find a microphone, speaker holes, and a USB-C port.

Dust & water resistance

The iPhone 15 Pro Max has an IP68 rating for water & dust resistance. The phone can withstand a depth of 6m (19.7ft) for about thirty minutes.

With an IP68 rating, the iPhone 15 Pro Max can withstand rain, accidental exposure to water, & splashes, but intentional exposure to water should be avoided.

Screen

The iPhone 15 Pro Max has an upgraded Super Retina OLED screen that spans the body of the smartphone. A contrast ratio of 2000000:1 allows for darker blacks & brighter whites, and the iPhone has a maximum brightness of up to 2,000 nits outdoors, which makes it easy to see your phone's display in the sun.

The iPhone 15 Pro Max has a 2796 x 1290 resolution with 460 pixels per inch.

Wide colour compatibility provides clear, life-like colours, & True Tone matches the screen's white balance to the lighting around the phone making the screen more pleasant to look at.

RAM

The iPhone 15 Pro Max has an 8GB RAM.

Storage space

The iPhone 15 Pro Max is available in 256 GB, 512 GB & 1TB storage options.

USB-C port

The new iPhone can now be charged with a USB-C cable.

USB-C allows your device to directly charge an Apple Watch or AirPod with a USB-C cable. Although the charging speed is slow, it is possible to charge another iPhone with the new iPhone 15 Pro Max.

Camera

The iPhone 15 Pro Max has an f/1.90 aperture front True-Depth camera that offers better performance for pictures & videos.

There's a 48MP Wide lens on the back of the iPhone 15 Pro Max, which makes use of 2nd-gen sensor-shift optical picture stabilization. The camera has a focal length of 24 mm and an aperture of f/1.780.

There's also an enhanced 12MP Telephoto camera on the back of the iPhone that offers 5x optical zoom.

Battery Life

The iPhone 15 Pro Max model is equipped with a 4422mAh battery. The iPhone 15 Pro Max can last about 29 hours when watching videos, about 25 hours when streaming videos, & about 95 hours when playing music.

SETUP YOUR IPHONE

Switch on your phone

Long-press your Phone's side button till the Apple symbol appears on the display.

Then you will see "Hello" displayed in many languages on your screen. Adhere to the directives on your screen to begin setup.

Choose the icons & text size on your phone

Dreg the slider to choose the icons & text size you want: Large, Medium, or Default. When you're done, touch the **Continue** button

Setup manually or use the Quick-Start feature

You can use the **Quick Start** feature to automatically set up your new iPhone if you have another device.

If you do not have other devices, click on the **Setup Without Another Device** button.

Activate your device

Your device has to be connected to a mobile or WiFi network to activate & proceed with the setup.

Touch one of the available WiFi networks to connect to it, or touch the **Continue without WiFi** option to utilize your iPhone's mobile network.

Setup for yourself or a child

Choose whether to setup the device for yourself or a child.

Setup Face ID & create a passcode

Adhere to the directives on your display to setup the Face ID feature so that you can use your face to unlock your phone & authenticate purchases.

After that, create a 6-digit passcode to protect your information. You need to set a passcode before you can use features like Apple Pay, Face ID, etc. Click on **Passcode Options** to see more options.

Restore or transfer your applications & data

Select how you want to move your data from your old device to your phone.

If there's no available backup or if you do not have other devices, click on the **Don't Transfer Anything** option.

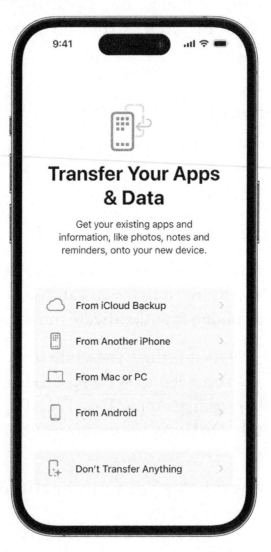

Log in with Apple ID

Fill in your Apple ID details in the appropriate fields, or touch the **"Forgot your password or don't have an Apple ID?"** option to create an Apple ID for yourself, setup Apple ID later, or recover your passcode or Apple ID.

If you have multiple Apple IDs, click on **Other Sign-In Options**, and then touch the **Use Multiple Accounts** button.

After signing in with your Apple ID, your phone might request for a verification code from your old device.

Activate automatic updates & setup other features

Adhere to the guidelines on your screen to allow your phone's OS to update automatically and setup other features, such as mobile service and Apple Pay or a phone number:

❖ You will be asked to setup or activate features & services such as Siri.
❖ Then, adhere to the directives on your display to configure Screen-Time, which shows how much time you spend on your device.
❖ Next, find out what information you can share with Apple & decide whether or not to share information with application developers.
❖ Touch Dark or Light to show a preview of how your device adjusts. Select the **Auto** option to set your phone to automatically switch between light & dark throughout the day. Touch the **Continue** button to finish the setup.

BASIC SETTINGS

iPhone 15 Pro Max

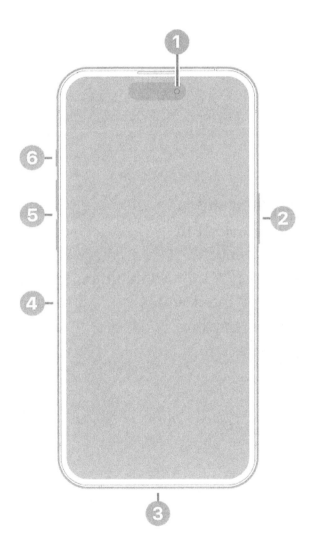

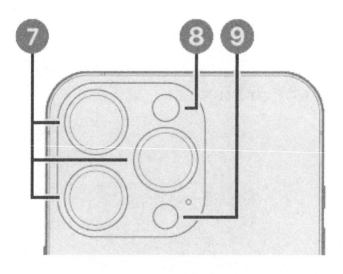

1) Front-facing camera
2) iPhone's Side button
3) USB-C connector
4) SIM card tray. Only available on models bought outside the United States.
5) The Volume button
6) Action button
7) Back camera
8) Flashlight
9) LiDAR Scanner

Wake your device

When your phone screen turns off, adhere to the directives below to wake it:

❖ Press your phone's Side button.

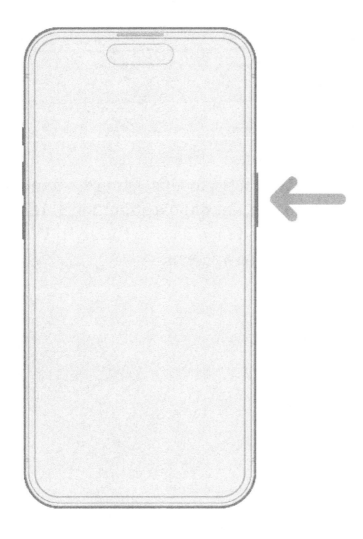

❖ Raise your device.

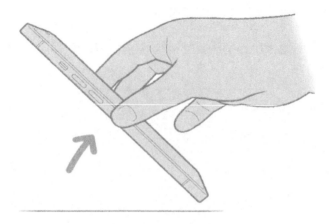

Note: To deactivate this feature, simply head over to the Settings application, touch Display & brightness, and then disable **Raise to Wake**.

❖ Tap your phone's screen.

Basic gestures

Use the following gestures to interact with your iPhone.

Hold down/long press: Use one of your fingers to press an item on your display till something happens. For instance, long-press the Home Screen's wallpaper to make the application icons jiggle.

Swipe: Move one of your fingers across your iPhone display quickly.

Scroll: Move one of your fingers across your phone display without raising it. For instance, in the Settings application, you can scroll up or down to check out more settings. Swipe to scroll faster; tap your phone's display to stop scrolling.

Zoom. Put 2 fingers close to each other on your display. Spread the fingers apart to zoom in, or drag the fingers close to each other or zoom out.

You can also double-tap a map or picture to zoom in, and tap it twice again to zoom out.

Go to the Home Screen: Swipe up from the lower edge of your phone screen to go back to the Home screen from any application.

Control Center: Swipe-down from the upper right edge of your display to enter the Controls Center. Hold down any of the controls to view options. You can remove or add controls, in the Setting application> Control Center.

Apps switcher: Swipe up from the lower edge of your phone display, and pause in the middle of the display. Swipe to the right to see all the open applications, and touch one of the applications to use it.

Move from one open app to another: Swipe right or left along the lower edge of your display to quickly move from one application to another.

Use Apple Pay. Press the side button twice quickly to show your Apple Pay default card, then stare at your phone screen to verify with Face ID.

Activate Siri: Say **"Hey Siri"** or **"Siri"**. Or press & hold the side button while making a request, then release the button when you are done.

Use Accessibility Shortcut. Press the Side button thrice quickly.

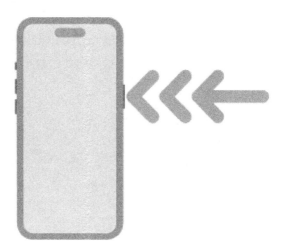

Use Emergency SOS. Hold down the side button & one of the volume buttons at the same time till you see the sliders and the Emergency SOS countdown ends, then release both buttons.

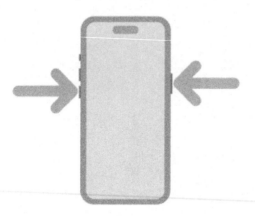

Turn off. Hold down the side button & one of the volume buttons simultaneously till the power off slider appears, then slide the Power off slider. Or head over to the Settings application, tap General, and then click on the **Shut Down** button.

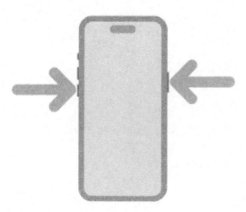

Force restart. Press & release the Increase volume button, press & release the Decrease volume button, and then hold down the Side button till you see the Apple symbol.

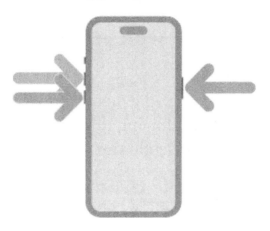

Unlock your iPhone with Face ID

If you activated Face ID when setting up your phone, adhere to the following directives to unlock your phone with Face ID.

❖ Press the side button or tap your display to wake your device, and then stare at the screen.
  The lock icon will animate from closed to open to let you know that your phone has been unlocked.
❖ Swipe up from the lower edge of your screen.

Press the side button to lock your phone. Your phone will automatically lock if the screen is not touched for about a minute.

Unlock your iPhone with passcode

If you created a password when setting up your device, adhere to the following directives to unlock your phone with the passcode you created:

❖ Press the side button or tap your screen to wake your device, then Swipe up from the lower edge of your phone's lock screen.
❖ Insert your passcode

Press the side button to lock your phone. Your phone will automatically lock if the screen is not touched for about a minute.

Find Settings on your phone

You can find the iPhone settings you want to change in the Settings application.

❖ Click on the Settings app's icon  in the Apps Library or your Home Screen.

❖ Swipe down from the upper part of the display to show the search box, then type a word—"Mail," for instance—then click on one of the settings that appear.

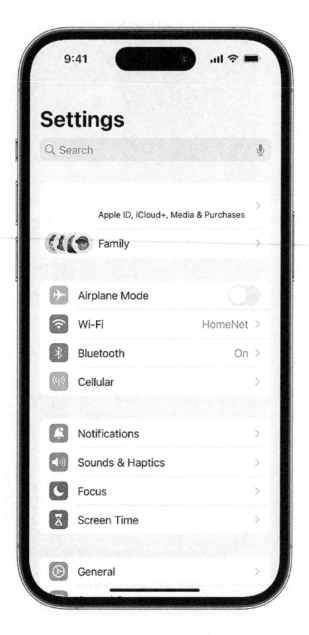

Set up an eSIM

Your device can store an eSIM provided by your carrier. If your SIM carrier allows eSIM Carrier Activation or eSIM Quick Transfer, you can switch on your new device and adhere to the directives to activate your eSIM when setting up your device.

If you've already finished setting up your phone, you can do any of the below:

❖ Activation of eSIM Carrier: Some carriers can assign a new eSIM to you; contact your SiM carrier to begin the process. When you get the "Complete Cellular Setup" notification, touch it. Or head over to the Setting application> Cellular, and then click on the **Add eSIM** button or the **Setup Cellular** button.

❖ Quick eSIM Transfer: Some SIM carriers allow users to transfer a phone number from their old phone to their new iPhone without contacting them. Ensure both devices are using iOS 16 or after.

On your new phone, head over to the Settings application> Cellular, click on the **Add eSIM** button or the **Setup Cellular** button, then click on the **Transfer From Nearby Phone** button or pick a phone number. Adhere to the guidelines on your old phone to confirm the transfer.

❖ Scan the QR code sent by your SIM carrier: Navigate to the Settings application> Cellular, click on the **Add eSIM** button or the **Setup Cellular** button, then select the **Use QR Code** option. (You may have to select Other Options first.) Set your phone in a way that the QR code can be seen clearly in the frame on your display, or fill in the info manually. You might be prompted to insert a verification code you received from your SIM carrier.

❖ Switched from a different phone: If your old device is not an iPhone, contact your carrier to transfer your number.

❖ Activate service from your SIM carrier's application: Launch the Apps Store on your iPhone, download your SIM carrier's application, and then activate mobile service in the application.

Install a physical SIM

❖ Put a SIM ejecting tool in the small hole of the SIM plate, and then push it inside the hole to bring the SIM tray out.

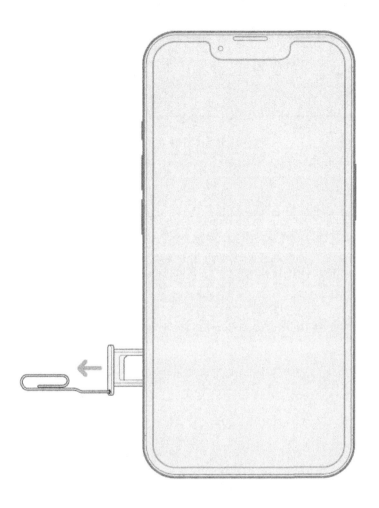

❖ Remove the SIM plate from the phone.
❖ Put your SIM card on the plate.

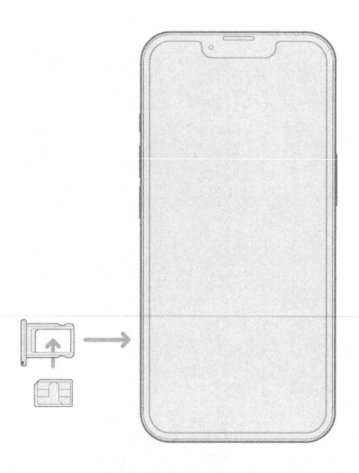

❖ Put the SIM plate inside your phone.
❖ If your SIM has a pin, insert the PIN correctly when told to.

Convert a Physical SIM to an eSIM

If your carrier allows it, follow the instructions below to convert your physical SIM to an eSIM.

❖ Navigate to the Setting application> Cellular, click on the **Setup Cellular** button or the **Add eSIM** button, and then select the number with a physical SIM.
❖ Click on the **Convert to eSIM** button, and then adhere to the guidelines on your display.

Setup Dual SIM

❖ Navigate to the Settings application> Cellular, then ensure there are 2 lines in the SIMs segment.
❖ Enable two lines — touch one of the lines, then click Turn On this Line.
❖ Pick the standard line for mobile data — Click on **Cellular Data**, and then click one of the lines. To use the two lines depending on availability & coverage, enable the **Allow Cellular Data Switching** feature.
❖ Select a standard line for calls—click on **Default Voice Line**, and then click on one of the lines.

Connect your device to the Internet

Use a Wifi or mobile network to connect your phone to the internet.

Connect to a Wifi network

❖ Navigate to the Settings application> WiFi, and then enable WiFi.
❖ Click on one of the below:
  ➢ A network: Type the passcode, if prompted.
  ➢ Other: To join a private network, type the network's name, security type & passcode.

If the Wi-Fi icon 📶 appears in the upper part of your display, it means your phone has connected to a WiFi network. (To confirm this, enter the Safari application and visit a website.)

Join a Personal Hotspot

If an iPad or iPhone is sharing Personal Hotspot, you can make use of its mobile Internet connection.

❖ Head over to the Settings application> WiFi, and then select the device that's sharing the Hotspot.

❖ If told to enter a password, simply insert the passcode displayed in the Settings application> Cellular> Personal Hotspot on the Personal Hotspot sharing device.

Connect to a mobile network

If WiFi is not available, your phone will automatically connect to your carrier's mobile data network. If your phone does not connect, check the following:

❖ Make sure your SIM is active & unlocked.
❖ Navigate to the Settings app> Cellular.
❖ Make sure Cellular data is enabled. If you are using two SIM cards, click on Cellular Data, then check the line selected.

Manage Apple ID settings

The account you use to gain access to Apple services (like iMessage, iCloud, Face-Time, Apps Store, etc.) is known as your Apple ID.

Log in with your Apple ID

If you did not log in when setting up your phone, do the following:

❖ Navigate to the Settings application.
❖ Click on **Sign in to iPhone**
❖ Fill in your Apple ID details.
  If you do not have an Apple ID, you can create one for yourself.
❖ If your account is protected with 2-factor authentication, type the 6-digit code.

Change your Apple ID settings

❖ Head over to the Settings application, and then click on [your name].
❖ Carry out any of the below:
  ➢ Update your profile
  ➢ Check & manage your subscriptions
  ➢ Remove or add account recovery contacts
  ➢ Change your login code
  ➢ Change your billing address or payment method
  ➢ Manage family sharing
  ➢ Use iCloud

Optimize iPhone battery charging

Your phone has a feature that helps slow battery aging by reducing charging time. The feature uses machine learning to understand your daily charging patterns, with this info it will make sure the battery does not charge above 80% till you need to use it.

❖ Enter the Settings application, touch Battery, and then touch Battery Health and Charging.
❖ Touch Charging Optimization, and then select Optimized Battery Charging.

iCloud

ICloud securely stores your files, backups, videos, pictures, etc. automatically. iCloud gives you 5GB of free storage space & an e-mail account.

Change iCloud settings

Log in with your Apple ID, and then carry out any of the below:

❖ Navigate to the Settings application, touch [your name], and then touch iCloud.

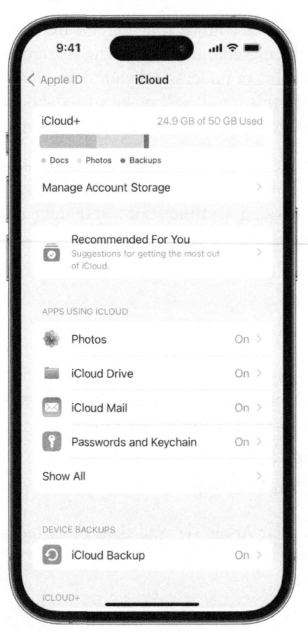

❖ Carry out any of the below:
  ➢ Check your iCloud storage space.
  ➢ Activate features you would like to use, like iCloud Mail, & Photos.

Upgrade, change, or cancel your iCloud+ subscription

❖ Enter the Settings application, touch [your name], and then touch iCloud.
❖ Click on the **Manage Account Storage** button, click Change Storage Plan, choose one of the options, and then adhere to the directives on your display.

Charge your phone with a cleaner energy source (United States only)

With the **Clean Energy Charging** feature, your phone makes use of a forecast of the carbon emissions in your local power grid to charge when cleaner energy is available. Your phone learns your daily charging pattern so it can be fully charged before you need it.

❖ Enter the Settings application, and then touch Battery.
❖ Touch Battery Health & Charging, and then activate the **Clean Energy Charging** feature.

Show your phone battery percentage

You can see how much charge your iPhone battery has in the status bar.

❖ Enter the Settings application> Battery and then activate Battery Percentage.
You will see the percentage in the battery symbol on the status bar in the upper part of your display.

Check the health of your phone battery

Navigate to the Settings application> Battery and then touch Battery Health & Charging.

Your phone will display info about your battery's peak performance, capacity, & whether it should be serviced.

View battery usage info

Enter the Settings application> Battery.

Use Low-Power Mode to reduce iPhone power consumption

Low power mode will reduce the power your iPhone uses when the battery is low. It improves the performance of critical tasks such as making calls; gaining access to the Internet; sending messages & e-mails; etc. When Low Power mode is activated, your phone may perform some functions slowly.

If your iPhone enters low power mode automatically, it will turn it off by itself when it charges to 80%.

Use any of the methods below to manually enable or disable Low Power Mode:

❖ In the Settings application: Enter the Settings application, touch Battery, and then activate or deactivate Low Power Mode.
❖ In the Controls Centre: Swipe-down from the upper right edge of your display to enter the

Controls Center, and then click on the Lower Power Mode button 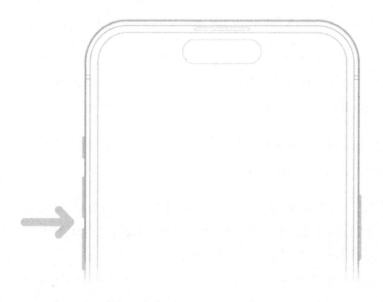.

(If the button is not in the Controls Centre, you can add it—simply launch the Settings application, touch Controls Centre, and then click the Add icon beside Low Power Mode.)

Change your phone's volume

Press the volume buttons on the side of your phone to change the volume level.

Change the volume level in the Controls Centre

To change the volume in the Controls Center, simply swipe-down from the upper right edge of your display to enter the Controls Center, and then drag the Volume slider 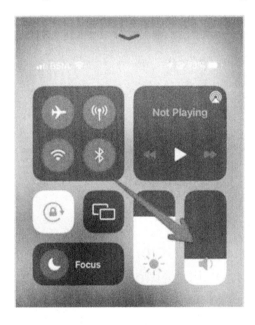 up or down.

Reduce loud headphone sounds

❖ Navigate to the Settings application, touch Sound and Haptics, and then click on Headphone Safety.

❖ Enable Reduce Loud Sound, and then slide the slider to set the maximum volume.

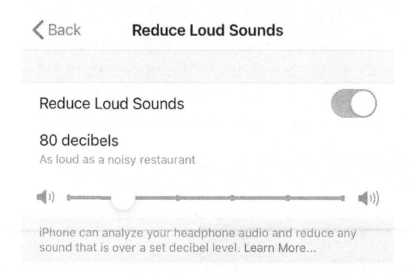

Temporarily silence notifications & calls

Swipe-down from the upper right edge of your display to enter the Controls Center, touch Focus, and then touch the **Do Not Disturb** option

Open applications on your device

You can launch Applications from the Apps Library or your Home Screen.

❖ To enter the Home screen, swipe up from the lower edge of your display.

❖ Swipe to the left to see applications on other pages of the Home Screen.
❖ Swipe to the left till you pass all the Home Screen pages before you can enter the Apps Library, where applications are arranged by category.

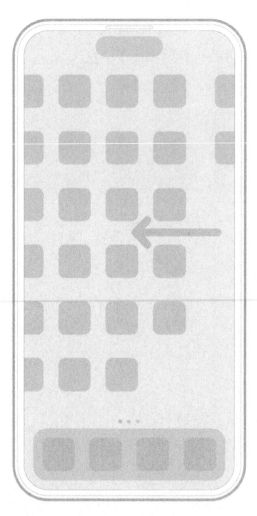

❖ Touch an application's icon to open it.
❖ To go back to the Apps Library, simply swipe up from the lower edge of your display.

Find applications in the Apps Library

The Apps Library displays your applications arranged into categories like Utilities, Information

& Reading, and Suggestions. Your most used apps are at the upper part of the display so that you can easily find & launch them.

Find & launch an application in the Apps Library

❖ Swipe up from the lower edge of your display to enter the Home Screen, then swipe to the left till you pass all the Home Screen pages before you can enter the Apps Library.
❖ Click on the search box, and then type an application name. Or scroll to check out the list.
❖ Touch an application to launch it.

Hide & show Home Screen pages

❖ Long-press the Home Screen's wallpaper till the applications starts jiggling.
❖ Click on the dot in the lower part of your display. Next, you'll see thumbnail pictures of your Home Screen pages with checkmarks under them.

❖ To hide Home Screen pages, touch to remove the check marks under the pages.
Touch to add the checkmarks to show the pages you've hidden
❖ Click on the **Done** button

Rearrange Home Screen pages

You can change the order of your Home Screen pages. For instance, you can put your favourite applications on one Home Screen page, and then make it your first page.

❖ Long-press the Home Screen till the applications starts jiggling.
❖ Touch the dots in the lower part of your display.

Next, you'll see thumbnail pictures of your Home Screen pages with checkmarks under them.

❖ To reorder the pages, simply long-press one of the Home Screen pages, and then drag it to another location on your screen.

❖ Touch Done two times.

Change where new applications get downloaded

When downloading new applications from the Apps Store, you can add the applications to the Apps Library & Home Screen, or just the App Library.

❖ Head over to the Settings application, and touch Home Screen
❖ Select one of the options to only show your new applications in the Apps Library or the Home Screen & Apps Library

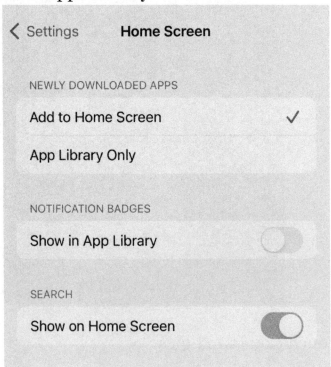

Application Switcher

Open the Apps Switcher to quickly move from one open application to another.

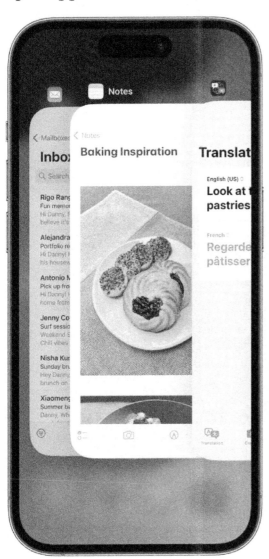

❖ Swipe up from the lower edge of your display, then stop in the middle of your display to show the Apps Switcher
❖ To view all your open applications, swipe right, and then touch one of the applications.

Move from one open app to another

Swipe right or left along the lower edge of your display to quickly move from one application to another.

Quit an application

Adhere to the directives below to quit an application:

❖ Swipe up from the lower edge of your display, and stop in the middle of your display to show the Apps Switcher.
❖ Swipe to the right to look for the application, and then swipe up on the application.

Multitask with Picture in Picture

With the Picture in Picture feature, you can make a FaceTime video call or watch a video clip while using other applications.

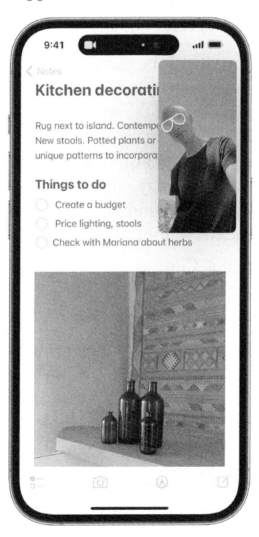

While watching a video, click on the Shrink Video icon .

The video window will scale down to one edge of your display so that you can see the Home Screen & launch other applications. With the video window showing, you can carry out any of the below:

❖ Change the size of the video window: Pinch open to make the video window bigger. Pinch closed to reduce the size of the window.
❖ Touch the window to display or hide controls.
❖ To move the window, simply drag it to any corner of your display.
❖ To hide the video window, simply drag it off any of the edges of your display.
❖ Click on the Close icon to close the video window.
❖ Go back to a full video screen: In the small video window, click the Full-Screen icon .

Access features from the Lock Screen

You'll see the Lock screen when you switch on or wake your phone. From your phone's Lock Screen, you can view notifications, enter the Camera application, get info from your favourite applications, control media play back, etc.

From the lock screen, carry out any of the below:

❖ Enter the Camera application: Swipe to the left. You can also long-press the Camera button 📷 , and then raise your finger.

❖ Enter the Controls Centre: Swipe down from the upper-right edge of your display.

❖ Swipe up from the middle of your display to view earlier notifications.

❖ Swipe right to see more widgets

❖ Use the media controls on your phone Lock Screen to fast-forward, rewind, pause, or play media on your device.

Display notification previews on your iPhone's Lock Screen

❖ Head over to the Settings application> Notifications.

❖ Click on the **Show Previews** button and then click on the **Always** button.

❖ Select how you want notifications to be displayed on your phone lock screen:

➢ Choose the **Count** option to show only the number of notifications.

> Select the **Stack** option to show the notifications grouped into stacks by application
> Choose the **List** option to show the notifications in a list.

Perform quick actions from the home screen & Apps Library

You can long-press an application in the Apps Library or Home Screen to open the quick actions menu.

For instance:

❖ Long-press the Notes app icon ', and then select New Note

❖ Long-press the Maps app icon ', and then select Search Nearby

❖ Long-press the Camera app icon and then touch Record Video.

Note: If you long-press an application for too long before selecting one of the quick actions, all the applications will start jiggling. Touch the **Done** button, and then try again.

Search with Spotlight

You can search for applications, contacts & contents in some apps on your device. You can also find & open websites, applications, and pictures in your photos library & on the internet.

Select which applications to include in Search

❖ Enter the Settings application> Siri & Search.
❖ Scroll down, touch one of the applications, and then enable or disable **Show App in Search**.

Search on iPhone

❖ Touch the Search button  in the lower part of your Home Screen.

❖ Type what you want in the search box.
❖ Carry out any of the below:
  ➢ Touch the Go or Search button to start your search.
  ➢ Touch one of the suggested websites to visit it

- Touch one of the suggested applications to open it.
- Learn more about a search suggestion: Touch it, and then touch a result to open it.
- Touch the Clear Text icon ⊗ to clear the search box

See the total storage and storage used for each application on your device

Enter the Settings application> General> iPhone Storage.

Learn more about your iPhone

Enter the Settings application> General> About

Activate Airplane mode

Swipe-down from the upper right edge of your display to enter the Controls Center, and then touch the **Airplane Mode** button ✈.

Tap to turn on
airplane mode.

You'll see the **Airplane Mode** button ✈ in the status bar when Airplane Mode is active.

Activate or deactivate WiFi or Bluetooth

❖ Swipe-down from the upper right edge of your display to enter the Controls Center

❖ Touch the WiFi button to activate WiFi or touch the Bluetooth button to activate Bluetooth

Tap to turn on Bluetooth.

Tap to turn on Wi-Fi.

Touch the WiFi button 🛜 to deactivate WiFi or touch the Bluetooth button ⁑ to deactivate Bluetooth in the Controls Center.

Tap to turn off Bluetooth in airplane mode.

Tap to turn off Wi-Fi in airplane mode.

Call an emergency number when your device is locked

❖ Touch the **Emergency** button on the Passcode screen

❖ Dial the emergency number(for instance, 911 in the United States), and then touch the Call button

Calculator

You can perform arithmetic, trigonometric, logarithmic, & exponential calculations in the Calculator application.

To use the scientific calculator, simply rotate your phone to landscape orientation.

Copy, clear, or delete numbers

❖ Copy calculation results: Long-press the calculation result on your screen, click on the **Copy** button, and then paste it in another application.

❖ To delete the last number, simply swipe right or left on your screen at the top.

❖ Clear the screen: Click on the Clear (C) button to clear the last entry or touch the **AC** button to clear all entries.

See the time in other cities around the world

You can check the time in different places around the world.

❖ Launch the Clock application, and then click on Work Clock.

❖ Carry out any of the below to manage your cities list:

> Add a city: Click on the Add button + and then select any of the cities.
> To delete one of the cities, simply touch the **Edit** button, and then touch the Remove icon ⊖
> Rearrange the cities: Click on the **Edit** button, and then drag the Rearrange button ≡ down or up.

❖ When you are done, touch the **Done** button.

Set an alarm

❖ Launch the Clock application, click on the **Alarm** button, and then click on the Add icon + .

❖ Set the time, and then select any of the options below:

> Repeat: Select the days you want the alarm to be active.
> Snooze: Give yourself some time to rest
> Sound
> Label

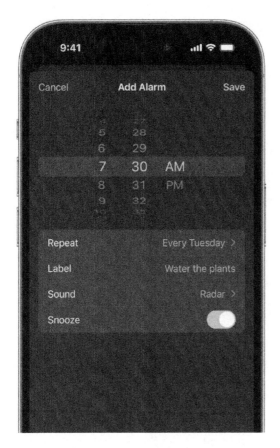

❖ Click on **Save**

Touch the alarm time to edit the alarm. Or touch the **Edit** button in the upper left part of the screen, and then click on the alarm time.

Click on the button beside the alarm time to deactivate the alarm

To delete an alarm, swipe the alarm to the left, and then touch the **Delete** button

Measure someone's height with your phone

You can use the Measure application to measure someone's height.

❖ Set your phone in a way that the person you want to measure can be seen clearly on your screen from head to toe.

   After a while, a line will appear on top of the individual's head, and the height measurement is displayed under the line.

❖ Click on the Capture button ○ to snap a picture of the measurement.

❖ To save the picture, click on the screenshot's thumbnail in the bottom left part of your display, touch Done, and then select one of the options to save it on your device.

Use your phone as a level

You can use your phone to check whether nearby objects are flat, straight, or level.

❖ Enter the Measure application.
❖ Touch the **Level** tab, and then hold your phone against an object, like a frame.
   ➢ Make an item level: Rotate your phone & the object till your display shows green.
   ➢ Match the slope: Touch your display to snap the slope of the first object. Hold your Phone firmly against the other object & move your

phone & the object till your display shows green.

Touch your display to reset the level.

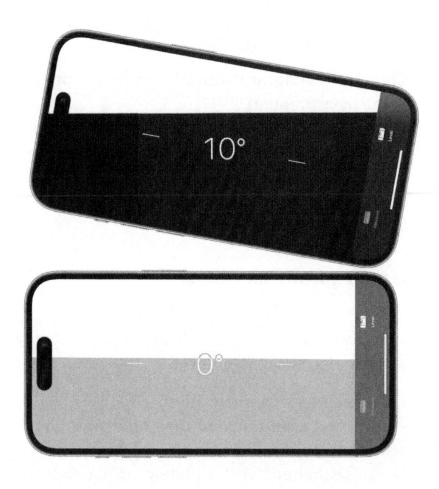

Use the compass on your device

The compass application shows you the direction your phone is pointing to, your location, and your altitude.

The bearings, coordinates, and altitude of your device are displayed at the lower part of your display.

Touch the coordinates at the lower part of your screen to show your location in the maps application.

DYNAMIC ISLAND

A Voice Memo
recording in progress

You can check notifications & current activities — like music playing, Voice Memos recording in progress, & Maps directions— in the Dynamic Island. The Dynamic Island can be found at the upper part of your display whenever your phone is unlocked.

You can carry out any of the below in the Dynamic Island:

❖ Enlarge the activity to view more details: Hold down the activity or swipe from the middle to the left or right side
❖ Move from one activity to another: Swipe from one side or the other
❖ Make the Dynamic Island smaller again: Swipe from the left or right side toward the middle.

PERSONALIZE THE ACTION BUTTON

Your new iPhone has an Action button instead of a Silent/Ring switch. You can select the function you want the button to perform when it's pressed.

Personalize the Action button

❖ Enter the Settings application, and then touch Action Button.
You will see a picture of the iPhone's side with icons that indicate actions you can perform with the Action button.

❖ To select one of the actions, simply swipe to the one you want—its name will appear under the dot.

❖ If there are more options for the action you picked, a Menu button ⌄ will appear under the action; Click to view a list of options.

For the Accessibility & Shortcut actions, you must click on the blue button under the action and choose one of the options—if not, the Action button won't perform any action.

CUSTOMIZE YOUR DEVICE

Change your iPhone vibrations & sounds

Change the sound your phone plays when you receive an e-mail, call, reminder, voicemail, or any other type of notification.

Set vibration & sound options

❖ Enter the Settings application and then touch Sound & Haptics.
❖ Move the slider in the Ringtone and Alert Volume section to set the volume for all sounds on your device.

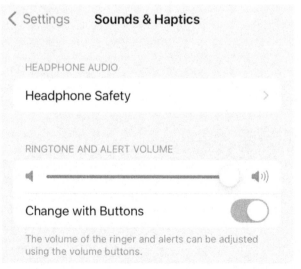

- ❖ To set the vibration & tones pattern for sounds, touch one of the sound types, like text tone or ringing tone.
- ❖ Carry out any of the below:
  - ➢ Choose one of the tones (scroll to view all of them).

    Ringing tones are for calls, clock timers, & alarms; text tones are for messages, voicemail, & other notifications
  - ➢ Click on Vibration, then select one of the vibration patterns, or click on the **Create New Vibration** button to create one for yourself.

Activate or deactivate Haptic feedback

- ❖ Navigate to the Settings application, and then touch Sound & Haptics.
- ❖ Activate or deactivate Systems Haptics

  When you deactivate System Haptics, you won't feel or hear vibrations from incoming notifications & calls.

Change your iPhone's wallpaper

❖ Enter the Settings application, touch Wallpaper, and then click on the **Add New Wallpaper** button.

Next, you'll see the wallpaper gallery

❖ Carry out any of the below:

   ➢ Touch one of the buttons in the upper part of the wallpaper gallery—like Live Photos, Photos Shuffle, etc.—to decorate your wallpaper with a picture, an emoji pattern, etc.

   ➢ Pick one of the wallpapers from any of the featured collections (Astronomy, Weather, etc.).

❖ Click on the **Add** button, and then carry out any of the below:

   ➢ Click on the **Set as Wallpaper Pair** option to use the wallpaper on your Lock & Home Screen.

   ➢ Make more adjustments to the Home Screen: Click on the **Customize Home Screen** option. Click on one of the colours to change the colour of the wallpaper, click on the Pictures icon to use one of your photos, or click on the **Blur** button to blur the wallpaper

Have your device play a sound effect when it is switched off & on

❖ Navigate to the Settings application, touch Accessibility, and then touch Audio/Visual.
❖ Activate or deactivate Power On & Off Sound.

Change the screen brightness manually

Adhere to the directives below to change your screen brightness manually:

❖ Swipe-down from the upper right edge of your display to enter the Controls Center, then drag the Brightness slide down or up.
❖ Navigate to the Settings application, touch Display & Brightness, and then slide the slider.

Enable or disable Dark Mode

The Dark mode feature gives your iPhone screen a dark colour scheme that is ideal for low-light environments.

Carry out any of the below:

❖ Swipe-down from the upper right edge of your display to enter the Controls Center, long-press the Brightness slide ☀, and then touch the Dark Mode button ◑ to activate or disable Dark Mode.

❖ Navigate to the Settings application, touch Display & Brightness, and then touch Dark to activate the Dark Mode, or touch Light to deactivate it.

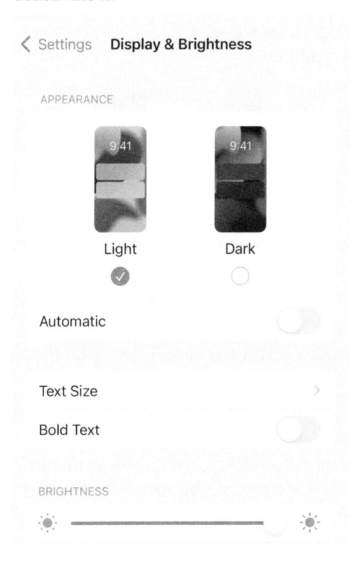

Adjust the screen brightness automatically

Your phone uses an inbuilt ambient light sensor to adjust the screen's brightness to the current lighting conditions.

❖ Enter the Settings application, and then touch Accessibility.
❖ Touch Display and Text Size, and then activate **Auto-Brightness**.

Set Dark Mode to activate or deactivate automatically

You can programme the Dark Mode to automatically activate at specific times (in the night or on a custom schedule).

❖ Navigate to the Settings application, and then touch Display & Brightness.
❖ Activate Automatic, and then touch Options.
❖ Touch **Custom Schedule** or **Sunset to Sunrise**.

If you pick Custom Schedule, click on the options to select when you want Dark Mode to activate & deactivate

If you pick Sunset to Sunrise, your device will use the info from your clock & location to determine when it is night for you.

Activate or deactivate Night Shift

The Night Shift feature can be useful when you are in a dark room during the day

Swipe-down from the upper right edge of your display to enter the Controls Center, long-press the Brightness button ☀ , then touch the Night Shift button ☀ .

Set Night Shift to activate or deactivate automatically

Set Night Shift to change the colours on your screen to the warmer side of the spectrum at night and make looking at the screen more pleasant to your eyes.

- Enter the Settings application, touch Display & Brightness, and then touch Night Shift.
- Activate **Scheduled**
- To change the colour balance for Night Shift, slide the slider in the Colour Temperature section to the cooler or warmer side of the spectrum.

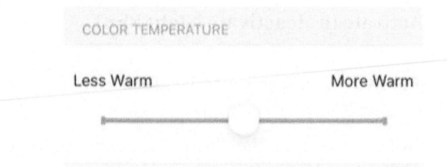

- Tap the **From** button, then touch **Custom Schedule** or **Sunset to Sunrise**.

  If you pick Custom Schedule, click on the options to select when you want Night Shift to activate & deactivate

  If you pick Sunset to Sunrise, your device will use the info from your clock & location to determine when it is night for you.

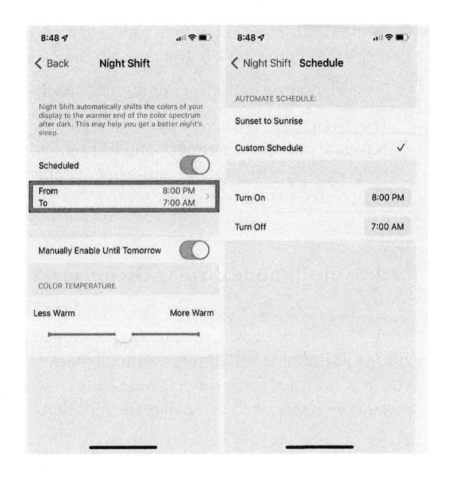

Activate or deactivate True Tone

True Tone automatically adjusts the display's colour & intensity to match the lighting around you.

Carry out any of the below:

❖ Swipe-down from the upper right edge of your display to enter the Controls Center, long-press the Brightness button ☀, and then touch the True Tone button ☀.
❖ Navigate to the Settings application, touch Display and Brightness, and then enable or disable True Tone.

Make your iPhone display On longer

Your phone screen will remain On while you are staring at it, but it will dim & eventually lock when you look away for some time. If you want the screen to stay On longer, you can change the duration.

Head over to the Settings application, click on Display and Brightness, click on the **AutoLock** button, then select the duration.

Always On Display

The Always On feature allows a darkened version of your Lock Screen to remain visible, even when your device is locked so that you can look at your screen any time to see important info, like the time, date, alerts, etc.

This feature is activated by default. To deactivate it, head over to the Settings application, click on Display and Brightness, then disable the Always On Display feature.

Use StandBy to check info at a distance while your device is charging

Use the StandBy feature to turn your device into a bedside clock, a digital picture frame, a Live Activities display, etc.

Start Standby

- ❖ Connect your device to power and place it on its side; make sure it's still.
- ❖ Press the side button
- ❖ You can swipe to the right or left to switch between clocks, pictures, & widgets. Swipe down or up to change the options for these views.

  In Night Mode, the display adapts to the dim light of the night and appears in a red tint so that it does not disturb you while you sleep.

Disable StandBy

Enter the Settings application, touch StandBy, and then deactivate the **StandBy** feature.

Increase the size of items on your screen

- ❖ Navigate to the Settings application, touch Display & Brightness, and then touch Display Zoom.
- ❖ Touch Lager Text to increase the size of the items on your screen.
- ❖ Touch Done in the upper right corner of your display, and then touch the **Use Zoomed** button.

Change your iPhone's name

You can change your iPhone's name, which is used by your Hotspot, AirDrop, your PC, & iCloud.

- ❖ Navigate to the Settings application, touch General, click on About, and then click on Name.
- ❖ Click the Clear Text button, type the name, and then click on Done.

Change the date & time on your phone

- ❖ Navigate to the Settings application, tap General, and then click on Date & Time.
- ❖ Activate any of the below:

➢ Set Automatically: Your device will get the accurate time over the network & your time zone.
➢ 24-Hour: Your device will show the hours from 0-23

To change the default time & date, deactivate **Set Automatically**, then change the time & date

Change the region & language on your device

❖ Navigate to the Settings application, click General, and then click on Language & Region.
❖ Set the following:
  ➢ Your phone's language
  ➢ How you would like to be addressed. (Select neutral, masculine, or feminine)
  ➢ Region
  ➢ Temperature unit
  ➢ Calendar format
  ➢ Measurement system
  ➢ Live text
  ➢ First day of the week

Organize your applications in folders

Arrange applications into folders to make it easy to look for them on your Home Screen.

Create folders

- ❖ Long-press the wallpaper of your Home Screen till the applications start vibrating.
- ❖ Drag one application unto another to create a folder.
- ❖ Drag more applications into the folder.
- ❖ To change the name of the folder, long-press the folder, click on **Rename**, and then type a name. If the applications start vibrating, touch the Home Screen, and try again.
- ❖ When you are done, click on **Done**, and then touch the Home Screen two times

To delete a folder from your device, open the folder, and then drag all the applications out of the folder. The folder will be erased automatically.

Move applications around your phone Home Screen

You can change your Home Screen's layout by moving applications around, dragging applications to other Home Screen pages, etc.

❖ Long-press an app's icon on your Home Screen, and then click on **Edit Home Screen.**
The applications will start vibrating.
❖ Drag an application to any of the locations below:
  ➢ Another Home Screen page

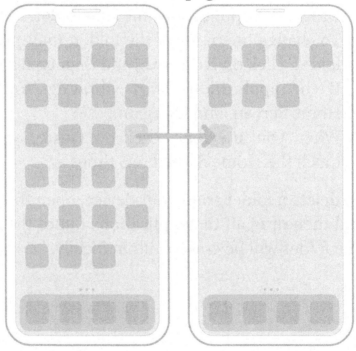

You can move an application to another page by dragging the application to the right edge of your Home Screen. You might have to wait for a few seconds for the next page to appear. The dots at the lower part of your Home Screen indicate how many pages you have & which one you are currently in.

➢ A different location on your same Home Screen
❖ When you are done, simply click on Done.

Reset the Home Screen & apps to their original settings

❖ Navigate to the Settings app, click on General, and then click on Transfer or Reset iPhone.
❖ Click on the **Reset** button, click on Reset Home Screen Layout, then click on the **Reset Home Screen** button
All the folders you have created will be deleted, and the applications you have downloaded will be arranged in alphabetical order after the applications that came with your device.

Uninstall applications from your phone

Carry out any of the below:

❖ Uninstall an application from your Home Screen: Press & hold the application on your Home Screen, click on the **Remove Apps** option, and then click on the **Remove from Home Screen** option to leave the application in the Apps Library, or click on the **Delete Apps** option to remove the application from your device.

❖ Remove an application from the Apps Library & Home Screen: Press & hold the application in the Apps Library, click on the **Delete Application** option, and then click on the **Delete** button.

Use & personalize the Controls Center

The Controls Centre on your phone gives you fast & easy access to useful controls like Media Control, Focus, the WiFi switch, & some applications.

To enter the Controls Centre, simply swipe down from the upper right edge of your display. Swipe up from the lower part of the screen to leave the Controls Centre.

Access more controls in the Control Center

A lot of controls have additional options. Press & hold one of the controls to view the available options. For example, you can:

Touch and hold to
see Camera options.

❖ Hold down the upper left set of controls, and then click on the AirDrop button to see the AirDrop options.

❖ Hold down the Camera button to snap a picture, or record a video.

Add & configure controls

Personalize the Controls Centre by adding shortcuts to applications & more controls.

❖ Navigate to the Settings app and then click on Controls Centre.

❖ Touch the Remove icon or the Add icon beside a control to remove or add a control

❖ To reorganize the controls, tap the Edit button beside a control and then drag the control to another location.

Disable access to the Controls Centre in applications

Navigate to the Settings app, click on Controls Centre, and then disable Access Within Apps.

Change or lock the screen orientation

Many applications look different when your device is rotated.

Lock the screen orientation so that it does not change when your device is rotated.

Swipe down from the upper right edge of your display to enter the Controls Center, and then click on the Screen Orientation button ⟳.

When you activate screen orientation, the Orientation Lock icon 🔒 will appear in the status bar.

Receive government alerts

In some countries, you can activate alerts in the Government Alert list. For instance, in the US, you can receive national alerts on your device.

❖ Navigate to the Settings application, and then touch Notifications.
❖ Scroll to the Government Alerts segment, and then activate any of them.

Type with your iPhone keyboard

You can use your phone keyboard to type & edit the text in applications.

In an application that supports text editing, tap the text field to bring out your iPhone keyboard, and then touch the individual buttons on the keyboard to type

While typing, you can do any of the below:

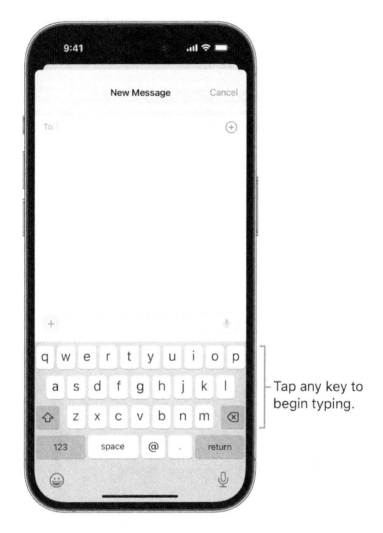

Tap any key to begin typing.

❖ Write Capital letters: Touch the Shift button⇧ then touch the letter.

❖ Activate Caps Lock: Tap the Shift button⇧ two times quickly.

❖ Insert symbols, punctuations, or numbers: Touch #+= or 123

❖ Insert an emoji: Touch the Emoji button 😃 to show the emoji keyboard

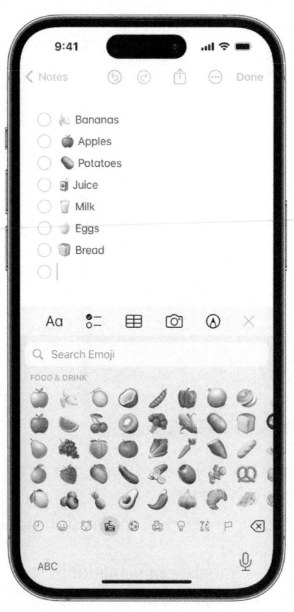

- ❖ Undo the last edit: Use 3 of your fingers to swipe left, and then click on the **Undo** button on your display.
- ❖ Redo the last edit: Use 3 of your fingers to swipe right, then click on the **Redo** button on your display.

Activate keyboard sounds & haptic feedback

Personalize keyboard settings to feel or hear tapping while typing.

- ❖ Enter the Settings application, touch Sound & Haptics, and then touch Keyboards Feedback.
- ❖ Activate Sound to hear tapping while typing; activate Haptic to feel tapping while typing.

Turn your phone keyboard to a trackpad

You can change your iPhone keyboard to a trackpad to easily move & set the point of insertion.

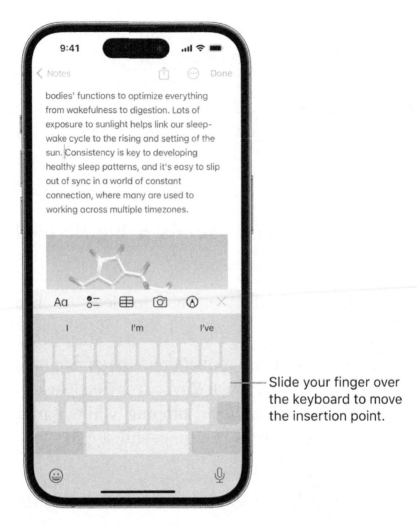

Slide your finger over the keyboard to move the insertion point.

❖ Use a finger to long-press the Space bar till the keyboard becomes light gray.
❖ Slide your finger around the keyboard to move the entry point.
❖ To highlight text, long-press the keyboard with a 2nd finger, then move your 1st finger around the keyboard to adjust the selection.

Move text

❖ In an application that supports text editing, highlight the text you would like to move.

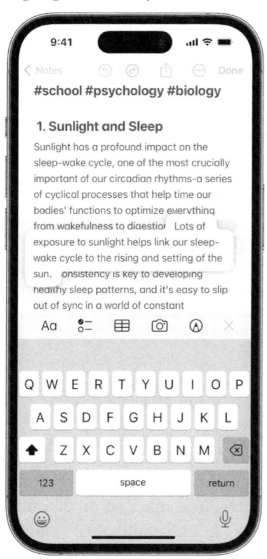

❖ Long-press the highlighted text till it lifts up, and then drag it to a different location in the application.

Dictation

You can dictate text anywhere you can type on your phone.

Activate Dictation

❖ Navigate to the Settings application, touch General, and then touch Keyboard.
❖ Activate **Enable Dictation.** If prompted, click on **Enable Dictation**.

Dictate text

❖ Touch to place the point of insertion when you want to enter text.
❖ Touch the Dictate button on your keyboard or in any field that it appears. Then start talking.
❖ To insert a punctuation mark or an emoji while dictating, simply say the name of the emoji (for

example smiley face emoji), or say the name of the punctuation mark (for example, Apostrophe)

❖ When you are done, touch the Dictation icon 🎤.

Deactivate Dictation

❖ Navigate to the Settings application, touch General, and then touch Keyboard.
❖ Deactivate **Enable Dictation**.

Select, cut, copy & paste text

❖ To highlight text in a text field, carry out any of the below:
   ➢ Double-tap a word to highlight the word.
   ➢ Tap a word in a paragraph three times quickly to highlight the paragraph.
   ➢ Select a block of text: Double-tap & hold the 1st word in the text block and then drag to the last word.
❖ Once you've selected the text you want to edit, you can type or touch the selection to display the editing options:

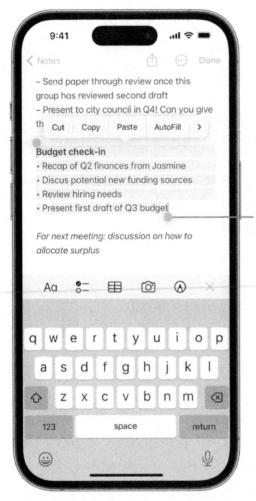

Move the grab points to adjust the selection.

- ➢ Copy: Click on the Copy button.
- ➢ Cut: Click on the Cut button
- ➢ Paste: Click on Paste
- ➢ Highlight all the text in the document: Touch the **Select All** button.
- ➢ Format: Change the formatting of the highlighted text.

➢ More Options icon ⟩: See more options

Save keystrokes with text replacement

Create text replacements that you can use to insert words or phrases by typing just a few letters. For instance, type "omw" to insert "on my way".

Adhere to the directives below to create a text replacement:

* ❖ While typing with your onscreen keyboard, long-press the Emoji key ☺ or the Globe key ⊕.
* ❖ Click on Keyboard Settings, and then click on Text Replacement.
* ❖ Click on the Add icon ✛.
* ❖ Type a phrase in the Phrases field, and type the shortcut in the Shortcut bar.

To change a word or phrase, simply enter the Settings application, touch **General**, touch **Keyboard**, touch **Text Replacement**, touch the Add icon ✛, and then type the phrase or word in the Phrases box, but leave the Shortcut field blank.

Switch to another keyboard

* ❖ While typing in a text field, hold down the Emoji key ☺ or the Globe button ⊕
* ❖ Touch the keyboard you would like to switch to.

Select a different keyboard layout

❖ Navigate to the Settings application, click on General, click Keyboard, and then click on Keyboards.

❖ Touch one of the languages in the upper part of your display, and then select one of the alternative layouts from the list.

Take a screenshot on your phone

Capture what's on your phone display so you can view it later, share it with other people, or add the image to documents.

❖ Press & release the side button and the increase volume button simultaneously.

The screenshot thumbnail will temporarily appear in the bottom left edge of your display.

❖ Touch the thumbnail to check the picture or swipe it to the left to remove it from your screen.

The Screenshots are automatically stored in the Photos application. To view all of them in one place, enter the Photos application, click on Albums, and then click on Screenshots in the Media Types section.

Take a full-page screenshot

You can capture a screenshot of content that's longer than the length of your iPhone's screen, like an entire webpage in the Safari application.

❖ Press & release the Side button and the Increase Volume button simultaneously.
❖ Touch the screenshot's thumbnail in the bottom left edge of your display.
❖ Touch the **Full Page** button, touch Done, and then carry out any of the below:
  ➢ Touch the **Save to Photos** button to store the screen-shot in the Photos application
  ➢ Touch the **Save to Photos** button, select a location, and then touch the **Save** button to store the screen-shot in the Files application.

Record what's on your screen

You can record what's happening on your phone screen.

❖ Navigate to the Settings application, touch Control Center, and then click on the Screen Recording icon ⊕ beside Screen Recording.
❖ Swipe down from the upper right edge of your display to enter the Controls Center, and then touch the Screen Recording button ⊙ .
  Your phone will start recording the screen after 3 seconds.
❖ To stop the screen recording, swipe down from the upper right edge of your display to enter the Controls Center, touch the Stop Recording button ⊚ , and then touch **Stop.**

The Screen recordings are automatically stored in the Photos application. To view all of them in one place, enter the Photos application, click on Albums, and then click on Screen Recording in the Media Types section.

Magnify items around you

In the Magnifier application, you can use your phone to zoom in on items around you.

❖ Enter the Magnifier application

❖ Drag the slider to the right or left to change the zoom level.

❖ Use any of the controls below:

> Touch the Brightness icon to change the brightness level.

> Touch the Contrast icon to change the contrast level of the item

> Touch the Filters icon to apply colour filters.

> Touch the Flashlight icon to turn on the flashlight.

> Touch the Lock icon to lock the focus

> Touch the Camera icon to switch to the back or the front-facing camera.

> Touch the Freeze icon to freeze the frame

> To freeze more frames, touch the Multi Photo Mode icon , and then touch the Add icon

To view the frames, click on the **View** button, and then touch the frames you would like to see. Touch the **Done** button or the Cancel icon to go back to the live lens.

Activate Screen Time & check your Screen Time summary

Use Screen Time to get info about how much time you spend on your device.

Enter the Settings application, touch Screen Time, touch Apps & Website Activity, and then touch Turn On Apps and Website Activity.

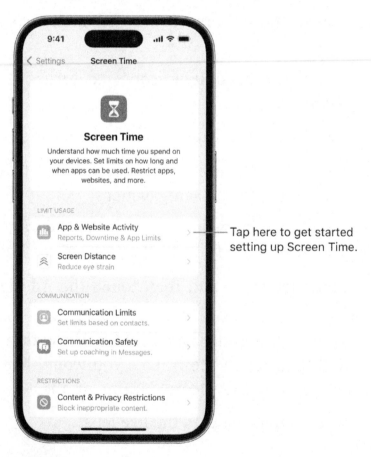

After activating Apps & Website Activity, you can see reports about your phone usage; including the amount of time you spend using certain types of applications, how often you use your phone, etc.

❖ Enter the Settings application, and touch Screen Time.
❖ Touch See All Apps and Websites Activity, and touch Devices to choose your device
❖ Touch Week to view your weekly summary or touch Day to view your daily summary

Create playlists on your phone

In the Music application, you can create a playlist & add songs that you can share with other people.

Create a playlist

❖ To create a playlist in the Music application, simply carry out any of the below:

  ➤ Touch the **Library** button, click on the **Playlist** button, and then touch **New Playlist**.

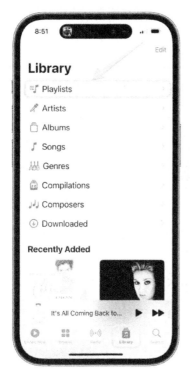

➢ Long-press an album, playlist, or song; click on **the Add to Playlists** button; and then click on the **New Playlist** button.

➢ On the Now Playing screen, click on the More Options icon●, click on the **Add to Playlists** button, and then click on **New Playlist**.

❖ Type a name & description to make it easy to identify the playlist.

❖ To give the playlist a cover art, click on the Camera icon📷, and then capture a picture or select one of the photos from your Photos Library.

❖ To add songs to your playlist, click on the **Add Music** button and then click on the search box, Library, Listen Now, or Browse button.

❖ Select or search for songs, and then click on the Add icon ⊕ to add the song to your playlist.

Edit your playlist

Click on the playlist, click on the More Options icon ⊙, and then carry out any of the below:

❖ Add songs: Click on the **Add Music** button, and then select songs.
You can also long-press an item (music video, playlist, album, or song), touch the **Add to a Playlist** button, and then select one of the playlists.

❖ Delete a song: Click on the Remove icon ⊖, and then click on the **Delete** button. Removing a song from your playlist does not remove the song from your library

❖ Rearrange the songs: Drag the Reorder button ☰ beside a song.

Sort your playlist

❖ Touch one of your playlists, and then click on the More Options icon ⊙ in the upper right part of your screen.

❖ Click on the **Sort By** button, and then select one of the options.

Delete a playlist

Press & hold the playlist, and then click on the **Delete from Library** button.

Or, touch the playlist, click on the More Options icon ⊙, and then click on the **Delete from Library** button

AirDrop

You can use AirDrop to wirelessly send videos, locations, sites, pictures, etc. to other Apple devices that are near you.

AirDrop moves data over WiFi & Bluetooth, so both must be enabled. You must sign in with your Apple ID to use AirDrop.

You can reject or accept requests as they arrive.

Send something via AirDrop

❖ Open the item you want to send on your phone, and then click on the Share icon⬆, the **Share** button, the **AirDrop** button, the More Options icon•••, or any other button that shows the application's sharing options.

❖ Touch the AirDrop icon◉, and then click on the AirDrop user you want to send the item to.

Tip: If you are near someone in your contacts list, you can open the file you want to share and then bring the iPhone closer to the contact's iPhone to initiate a transfer.

If the individual does not appear on your device as an AirDrop user, tell the person to open the Controls Centre on their device & let AirDrop receive items. If you want to send an item to a Mac user, tell the person to allow themselves to be discovered in AirDrop in the Finder.

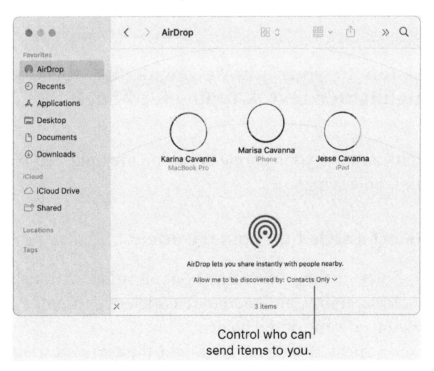

Control who can send items to you.

Let others send things to your phone via AirDrop

❖ Swipe down from the upper right edge of your display to reveal the Controls Centre, press & hold the upper-left set of controls, and then touch the AirDrop icon .

❖ Touch **Everybody for Ten Minutes** or **Only Contacts** to select who you would like to get items from.

Listen to your phone speak the screen, highlighted text, & typing feed-back

You can have your phone speak highlighted text or the whole screen.

Select a style for spoken content

❖ Enter the Settings application, touch Accessibility, and then touch Spoken Content.

❖ Activate any of the below:
  ➢ Speak Selection: Highlight the text you want to be read out.

- Speak Screen: Have your device read out everything on your display.
- Speech control: Display the Speech controller for easy access to the Speak Screen.
- Highlight content: Your phone can highlight words as they are spoken.
- Typing Feedback: You can set typing feedback for your keyboard and choose to have your phone read out each character, whole words, auto-caps, etc.

   To hear typing predictions, you also have to head over to the Settings application, tap General, tap Keyboards, and then activate **Predictive**.
- Voice: Pick a voice & accent.
- Slide the slider to set the speaking rate
- Pronunciation: Dictate or spell how you want your phone to pronounce certain sentences.

Hear your phone speak

You can summon Siri and then say "Speak Screen".

You could say "Hey Siri Speak Screen"

Or carry out any of the below:

- ❖ Hear highlighted text: select a word or paragraph, and then click on **Speak**.
- ❖ Hear the whole screen: Use 2 of your fingers to swipe down from the upper edge of your display. Use the visual controls to pause the speech or adjust the speed.
- ❖ Hear typing feed-back: Start typing. Press & hold each word to hear typing predictions (when activated).

Back Tap

The Back Tap feature allows your device to perform a specific action—like capturing a screenshot, activating an accessibility feature, etc.—when you triple-tap or double-tap the back of your phone

- ❖ Navigate to the Settings application, touch Accessibility, tap **Touch**, and then click on Back Tap.
- ❖ Touch Triple-Tap or Double-Tap, and then select one of the actions.
- ❖ Triple-tap or double-tap the back of your phone to perform the action you set.

To deactivate the Back Tap feature, navigate to the Settings application, touch Accessibility, tap **Touch**, click on Back Tap, touch Double Tap or Triple Tap, and then click on **None**.

Turn off all vibrations on your phone

Navigate to the Settings application, touch Accessibility, tap **Touch**, and then deactivate Vibration

Reachability

With Reachability, you can lower the top half of your display so that you can easily reach it with your thumb.

❖ Navigate to the Settings application, touch Accessibility, tap **Touch**, and then activate Reachability
❖ Swipe down from the lower edge of your display to lower the upper half of your display.
❖ Touch the top half of your display to go back to full screen.

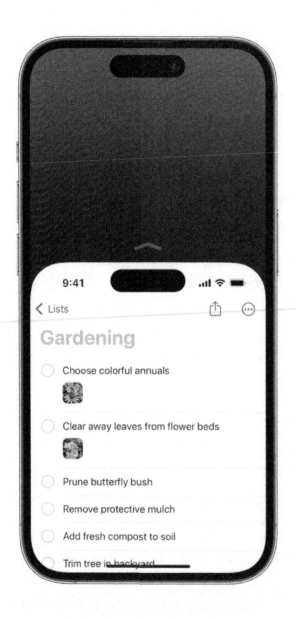

Use your device as a remote microphone

The Live Listen feature allows you to stream sound from the MIC on your phone to your AirPods or other hearing devices. This can be very helpful when you are discussing in a noisy place.

❖ Connect your AirPods to your phone and put them on your ears.
❖ Carry out any of the below to activate or deactivate the Live Listen feature:
  ➢ Swipe down from the upper right edge of your display to reveal the Controls Centre, touch the Hearing Devices button , touch your AirPods or a hearing device, and then click on the **Live Listen** button.
  (If you can't find the Hearing Devices button in the Controls Centre, you can add it— simply enter the Settings application, touch Controls Centre, and then click on the Add icon beside Hearing.)
  ➢ If you are making use of a hearing aid, enter the Settings application, touch Accessibility, touch Hearing Devices, and then activate Live Listen.
❖ Place your phone very close to the sound source.

Type-to-speak with Live Speech

The Live Speech feature allows you to type & have your words spoken in person & on calls

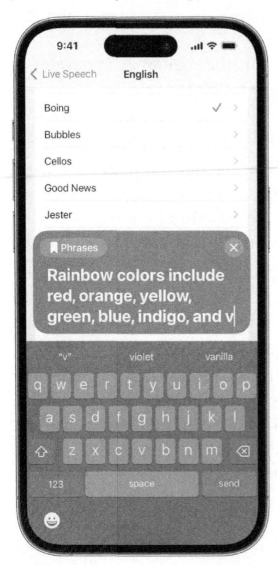

❖ Navigate to the Settings application, touch Accessibility, touch Live Speech, and then activate Live Speech.
❖ Choose one of the voices.
❖ Press the side button three times quickly, enter text in the text field, and then touch the **Send** button to have your text read out.

INTERACT WITH TEXT & SUBJECTS IN PICTURES

Live Text

When viewing a picture or when you Pause a video in the Photos application, Live Text identifies the text & info in the picture, allowing you to interact with it in many ways. You can highlight text to translate, share, copy, and more.

Enable Live Text

Before you use Live Text, ensure you've activated it for all supported languages.

- ❖ Navigate to the Settings application, touch General, and then touch Language & Region.
- ❖ Enable the **Live Text** feature.

Use Live Text

❖ Open an image or pause a movie that has text in it.

❖ Click on the Live Text button ⬚, then long-press the highlighted text.

❖ Select the text you want using the grab points, and then carry out any of the below:
  ➢ Copy text: You can paste the copied text in other applications.
  ➢ Click on the **Select All** button to select every text in the frame.
  ➢ Touch the **Lookup** button to see specific website suggestions.
  ➢ Touch the **Translate** button to translate the selected text.
  ➢ Search the web: Get more info about the selected text on the internet.
  ➢ Touch the **Share** button to share text using any of the sharing options.
❖ Touch the End Live Text icon to go back to the video or picture.

Perform a task within a video or picture

Depending on what's in the video or picture, you can touch one of the quick actions at the lower part of your display to do things like convert currencies, translate languages, receive directions, make a call, etc.

❖ In the Photos application, open an image or pause a movie that has text in it.

❖ Click on the Live Text button ⌞☰⌟

❖ Touch one of the quick actions in the lower part of your display.

❖ Touch the End Live Text icon ⬤ to go back to the video or picture.

Visual Look Up

Use Visual Lookup to identify objects in a picture and get more information about famous places, animals, plants, etc.

Visual Look Up
is available.

❖ Open a picture or pause a video.

If you see the Information icon ⓘ or 🐾 in your display, it means Visual Lookup is available.

❖ Click on the Visual Lookup icon, and then touch Lookup in the upper part of the picture info to see the Visual Look Up results.

❖ Click on the Close icon ✕ to close the Visual Lookup results.

Isolate a subject from the video or picture background

In the Photo application, you can remove the subject of a video or picture from its background, and then share or copy it.

❖ Open a picture or pause a video.
❖ Long-press the subject. Carry out any of the below when you see an outline around the subject:
  ➢ Keep tapping the subject, and then open a document in another application with another finger & drag the subject into the document.

> Click on the Copy button, and then paste the subject into a note, text message, or e-mail.

- ➢ Click on the **Lookup** button to see results & get more info about the subject.
- ➢ Click on the **Add Stickers** button, and then store the sticker for use in pictures, e-mails, messages, etc.
- ➢ Click on the **Share** button, and then select one of the sharing options.

PERSONALIZE THE LOCK SCREEN

You can customize the Lock Screen by picking a wallpaper, displaying a favourite picture, changing the time's font, etc.

Customize a new Lock Screen

❖ Long-press the Lock Screen till you see Customize & an Add icon ⊕ in the lower part of your display.
If they do not appear, long-press the Lock Screen once more, and then type your password.

❖ Touch the Add icon⊕ to create a new lock screen, or change some things in a Lock Screen, swipe to the screen you would like to edit, click on the **Customize** button, and then click on the **Lock Screen** button.

❖ If you want to create a new Lock Screen, touch any of the wallpapers to select it as your Lock Screen.

❖ Touch the time to change its style, colour, & font. Slide the slider to make the font lighter or thicker.

❖ To add widgets that have info like weather reports, or today's headline, simply touch the

Add Widgets button, the date, or the box under the time.

Tap to add widgets to your Lock Screen.

❖ Click on the **Done** button or the **Add** button, and then touch the **Set as Wallpaper Pair** or the **Customize Home Screen** button.

➤ Click on the **Set as Wallpaper Pair** option to use the wallpaper on your Lock & Home Screen.
➤ Make more adjustments to the Home Screen: Click on the **Customize Home Screen** option. Click on one of the colours to change the colour of the wallpaper, click on the Pictures icon to use one of your photos, or click on the **Blur** button to blur the wallpaper

Personalize your Lock Screen photo

If you select a picture for your Lock Screen, you can customize it to fit your style.

Carry out any of the below:

❖ Reposition the picture: To reset the picture you've selected, pinch open to zoom in on the picture, drag the picture with 2 fingers to move it, and then pinch closed to zoom out.
❖ Use a different style for the picture: Swipe to the right or left to check out different photos style with additional colour filters & fonts.
❖ Create a multi-layered effect: If the picture is compatible with layering—like a picture with

animals, or the sky/clouds— click on the More Options icon ⬤ in the lower right part of your display, and then click on the **Depth Effects** button.

❖ Create motion effects with a Live Photo: If you selected a Live Photo that can be played in slow motion, touch the Play icon ▶ in the lower part of your display to play the live photo anytime you wake your phone.

❖ Set the switching frequency: If you select the Photos Shuffle option, you can browse the pictures by clicking on the Browse icon ⬛, and you can set the switching frequency by clicking on the More Options icon ⬤, and then choosing one of the options under Shuffle Frequency.

Tip: You can also add a picture from the Photos Library to your Lock Screen & Home Screen. In the Photos application, touch the **Library** tab, select one of the pictures, and then touch the Share icon ⬆. Scroll down, touch the **Use as Wallpaper** button, touch the **Add** button, and then click on the **Set as Wallpaper Pair** option to use the wallpaper on your Lock & Home Screen.

Link a Focus to your Lock Screen

The Focus feature helps iPhone users to focus their attention on a task by reducing distractions. You can setup a Focus to temporarily mute all notifications/alerts or allow only certain alerts/notifications (for instance, notifications related to the task you are working on). When you link a Focus to your Lock Screen, the Focus Setting will activate anytime you make use of that Lock Screen.

❖ Long-press the Lock Screen till you see the **Customize** button in the lower part of your display.
❖ Click on the Focus button in the lower part of the wallpaper to view the Focus modes—for instance, Work, Sleep, & DND.

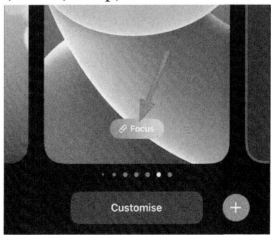

❖ Choose one of the Focus options, and then touch the Close icon .

Customize or change your Lock Screen

After creating a custom Lock Screen, you can edit it.

❖ Long-press the Lock Screen till you see the **Customize** button & the Add icon in the lower part of your display.
If they do not appear, long-press the Lock Screen once more, and then type your password.

❖ Swipe to the lock screen you would like to edit, click on the **Customize** button, and then click on the **Lock Screen** button.

❖ Touch the time to use a different colour, style, & font.

❖ To add widgets that have info like weather reports, or today's headline, simply touch the **Add Widgets** button, the date, or the box under the time.

❖ Click on the **Done** button or the **Add** button, and then touch the **Set as Wallpaper Pair** or the **Customize Home Screen** button.

Move from one Lock Screen to another

You can create multiple Lock Screens and then move from one to another anytime you like

❖ Long-press the Lock Screen till you see the **Customize** button in the lower part of your display.
❖ Swipe to the lock screen you would like to use, and then touch it.

Delete a Lock Screen

❖ Long-press the Lock Screen till you see the **Customize** button in the lower part of your display.
❖ Swipe to the Lock Screen you would like to erase, swipe up on the Lock Screen, and then touch the Delete icon .

SIRI

With Siri's help, you can perform tasks on your phone using your voice. You can use Siri to get weather reports, find locations, set alarms, translate a sentence, etc.

Siri responds to a request for an alarm at 8:00 AM.

Indicates that Siri is listening.

Setup Siri

If you did not configure Siri when setting up your device, simply carry out any of the below:

❖ If you would like to use your voice to activate Siri: Head over to the Settings application, touch Siri & Search, touch the "Listen for" button, and then select "Siri" or "Hey Siri"

❖ If you would like to use a button to activate Siri: Navigate to the Settings application, touch Siri & Search, and then activate Press Side Button for Siri.

Activate Siri

Long-press the Side button or say "Hey Siri" or "Siri" and then make a request.

For instance, you could say "Hey Siri, what is the weather report for tomorrow"

Type instead of talking to Siri

- ❖ Navigate to the Settings application, touch Accessibility, touch Siri, and then enable the **Type to Siri** feature.
- ❖ To make a request, summon Siri, and then type your request in the text field

Tell Siri about yourself

For a more personalized experience, you can give Siri info, including your relationship details, and your home & work address, so you can say things like "Give me directions to my house" & "Face-Time dad."

Tell Siri who you are

- ❖ Enter the Contacts application, touch **My Cards** in the upper part of your display, touch the **Edit** button, and then fill in your contact info.
- ❖ Enter the Settings application, touch Siri & Search, touch My Info, and tap your name.

Tell Siri about a relationship

You could say "Hey Siri, Herbert Clark is my husband" or "Hey Siri, Philip Damian is my father"

Announce calls

With the Announce Call feature, Siri can identify an incoming Face-Time or phone call, which you can use your voice to decline or accept.

❖ Navigate to the Settings application, touch Siri & Search, touch Announce Calls, and then select one of the options.
❖ When someone calls your device, Siri will identify the caller, and ask if you would like to take the call. Say **Yes** to take the call or **No** to reject it.

Change when Siri responds

Navigate to the Settings application, click on Siri & Search, and then carry out any of the below:

❖ Deactivate the **Listen for "Hey Siri"** to stop your device from responding to the "Hey Siri" voice request.

* Deactivate the **Press Side Button for Siri** to stop Siri from responding to the side button.
* Deactivate **Allow Siri When Locked** to disable access to Siri when your device is locked.
* Change the language Siri responds to: Click on Language, and then choose one of the languages.

Change Siri's voice

* Navigate to the Settings application, and then touch Siri & Search.
* Touch Siri Voice, and then select one of the voices.

Change how Siri responds

Navigate to the Settings application, click on Siri & Search, and then carry out any of the below:

* View your request on the screen: Touch **Siri's Response**, and then activate **Always Show Speech**

- ❖ Always show Siri's response on your screen: Touch Siri Response, and then activate Always Show Siri Captions
- ❖ Change when Siri responds by voice: Click on Siri Responses, and then select one of the options in the Spoken Response section.

SAFETY FEATURES

Use Emergency SOS via satellite

You can access emergency services via satellite if you don't have cellular or WiFi coverage.

Before disconnecting from mobile networks & WiFi

If you're traveling to a location that may not have mobile & Wifi coverage, setup your Medical ID, add emergency contacts, and then try the Emergency SOS demo before leaving.

- ❖ Navigate to the Settings application, and touch Emergency SOS.
- ❖ Scroll down and touch the **Try Demo** button.

Connect to emergency SOS via satellite

You can use Emergency SOS via satellite to contact emergency services if you are in a location that does not have a mobile or WiFi connection.

❖ Call 911 or any other emergency number you know. Even if you do not have a regular cellular network, your device will try to call 911 through another network.

❖ If it does not go through, touch the **Emergency Text via Satellite** button to text the emergency department.

❖ Click on the **Report Emergency** button and then adhere to the directives on your display.

Important: To connect to a satellite, simply hold your phone in your hand—you do not need to raise your phone up, just ensure your phone is facing the sky. If you are surrounded by thick foliage or other obstacles, you may not be able to connect to the satellite.

After connecting, your device will start a text conversation by sharing important info like your Medical ID & emergency contact details (if you've set them up), your answer to the emergency questions, your location, and the battery level of your device.

Ask for roadside assistance via satellite

If you are in a location that does not have mobile or WiFi coverage, you can request Roadside Assistance via satellite.

Get roadside assistance via satellite

❖ Enter the Messages application on your phone.

❖ Click on the Compose icon  in the upper part of your display, and then type **"roadside"** in the address box.

❖ Touch the **Roadside Assistance** button, and then adhere to the directives on your display.

Important: To connect to a satellite, simply hold your phone in your hand—you do not need to raise your phone up, just ensure your phone is facing the sky. If you are surrounded by thick foliage or other obstacles, you may not be able to connect to the satellite.

After connecting, you will be asked for important info, like your car model, and the problem you are experiencing. They will also ask if you are already a AAA(American Automobile Association) member, so please ensure you have your AAA info with you. If you aren't a AAA member, you can still receive help.

After answering the questions, you will be told how to connect to the satellite and you will be able to communicate directly with the roadside assistance provider. They may ask you some follow-up questions to ensure they send you the right help. You can contact them with any questions about how long it will take for someone to arrive and how much the service will cost you.

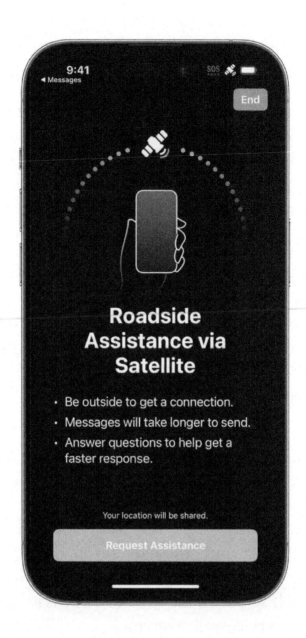

Create & check out your medical ID

Page | 176

Your Medical ID gives important info about you that might be useful in emergency situations, such as emergency contact info, allergies, etc. Your phone can provide this info to the individual attending to you in an emergency situation.

Set up your medical ID

Setup a Medical ID in the Health application.

❖ Head over to the Health app.
❖ Click on your picture in the upper right part of your display, and then click on the **Medical ID** button
❖ Click on **Get Started** or **Edit**, and then insert your info
❖ In the Emergency Contact segment, click on the **Add Emergency Contact** button, and then add the contacts
After ending an emergency call, your device will alert your emergency contacts via text message unless you decide to cancel. Your phone will send your location.
❖ Click on Done.

Tip: To see your Medical ID from your phone's Home screen, hold-down the Health app's icon, and then select the **Medical ID** option.

Let emergency services & first responders gain access to your Medical information

❖ Launch the Health application on your phone.

❖ Click on your photo in the upper right corner of your display, and then click on Medical ID.

❖ Click on the **Edit** button, scroll down, and then activate the **Show When Locked & Emergency Call** feature.

Note: First responders can find your Medical ID from your phone Lock Screen by swiping up, clicking the **Emergency** button in the passcode display, and then clicking on the **Medical ID** button.

Use Check-In to let your friends know that you have arrived

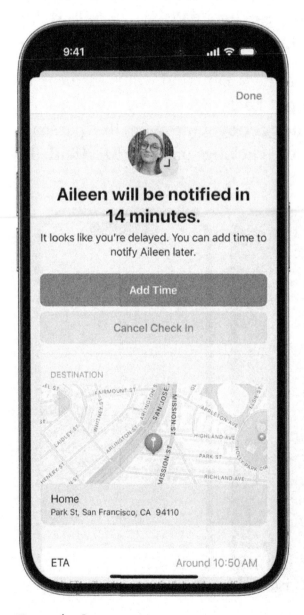

The **Check-In** feature allows your phone to notify a friend when you arrive at a specified location at a set time. You can also choose which information they can see if you do not get to the location at the time you set.

Likewise, if a friend sends you a Check-In but they haven't arrived as expected, you can see their location, mobile signal, phone battery percentage, etc.

Send a Check In

❖ Enter the Messages application.

❖ Touch the Compose icon ☑ and add a recipient, or choose one of the existing conversations.

❖ Click the Add icon ✛ , and then click on the **More** button

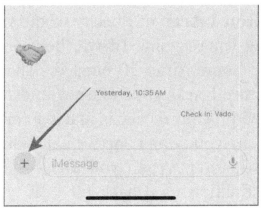

❖ Click on the **Check In** button, and then click on the **Edit** button.

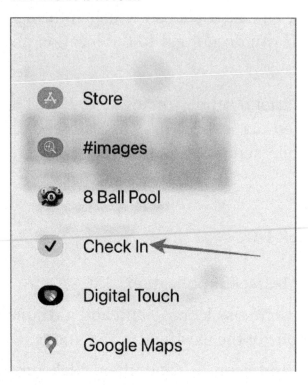

❖ Select any of the below:

➢ **When I Arrive:** Specify where you're going, how you're going (drive, bus, or walk), and add more time if needed. The **Check-In** feature tracks your journey and notifies your friend if your device is inactive for a long time or if you don't arrive at your expected destination. When you arrive safely at your destination, Check-In is completed automatically and your friend will receive a notification that you have arrived at your destination.

➢ **After the timer:** Set a time—for instance, if you are meeting someone new. If you do not end the Check-In before the scheduled time, Check-In will send your friend a notification.

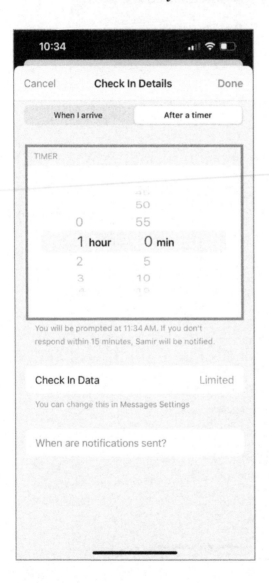

❖ Click on the send icon ⬆ .

If your phone does not get to your destination or you do not cancel Check-In, and you do not respond to Check-In messages, your phone's journey information will be sent to your friend.

Add more time to your Check In

If you need more time, simply follow the instructions below:

❖ Enter the Message application.
❖ Open the conversation with the individual you sent a Check In to.
❖ In the Check In message, click on the **Details** button, touch the **Add Time** button, and then choose an option.

Cancel a Check In

If you have arrived at your destination or want to end the session, you can cancel your Check In message.

❖ Enter the Message application.

❖ Open the conversation with the individual you sent a Check In to.

❖ In the Check-In message, click on the **Details** button, then touch the **Cancel Check-In** button

Choose what information you share

❖ Enter the Message application.

❖ Scroll down and then touch the **Check-In Data** button

❖ Select the information you would like to share if you do not finish your Check In as expected:

  ➢ When I Arrive: Share your location plus battery percentage & network signal.

  ➢ Full: Share the above information (network signal, current location, & battery information) in addition to your journey and the last time you unlocked your phone.

Crash Detection

If a serious car accident is detected by your device, it can help you contact the emergency department

& inform your emergency contacts about your situation.

How Crash Detection Function

If your device detects a serious accident in your car, it'll show a notification and automatically start calling emergency services after twenty seconds if it is not canceled. If you're unresponsive, your smartphone will play a voice message for the emergency department, informing them that you have been in an accident & and giving them your location details.

If you are involved in a severe car accident & unresponsive in a place that does not have a mobile or WiFi connection, your device will try to contact emergency services via SOS via satellite if possible.

Activate or deactivate Crash Detection

Crash Detection is activated by default. You can deactivate it in the Settings application, click on Emergency SOS, and then deactivate the **Call after Severe Crash** feature.

Reset your security & privacy in an emergency

The Safety Check feature allows you to quickly stop sharing your phone access & personal details with other people. This feature helps iPhone users to quickly change their phone passcode & Apple ID login code, stop sharing their location via Find My, etc.

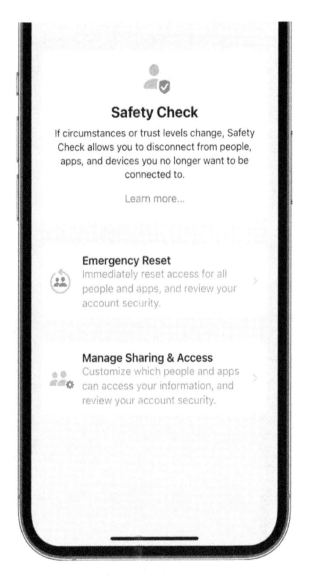

- ❖ Navigate to the Setting app, click on Privacy and Security, and then click on Safety Check.
- ❖ Click on the **Emergency Reset** button, click **Start Emergency Reset**, and then adhere to the directives on the screen

With the Safety Check feature, you can also periodically review & make changes to the details you share with other devices, applications, & individuals.

DOWNLOAD APPLICATIONS FROM THE APP STORE

You'll find new applications, exclusive stories, tips and tricks, and in-application events in the Apps Store application 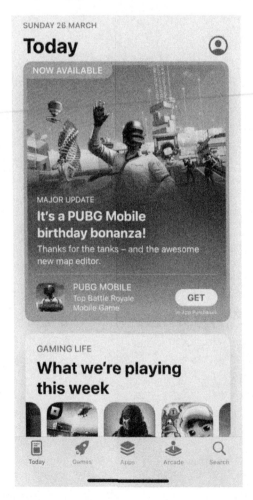.

Note: Your device has to be connected to the internet before you can use the Apps Store.

Find applications

Click on any of the below:

- ❖ Today: Explore stories, applications & in-application events.
- ❖ Games
- ❖ Apps.
- ❖ Arcade: Enjoy premium games from Apple Arcade (subscription required) without advertisements or in-application purchases.
- ❖ Search.

Get more information about an application

Touch an application to find the following info & more:

- ❖ In-apps event
- ❖ Size of the file
- ❖ Reviews & ratings

- ❖ Previews or screenshots
- ❖ Support for other Apple devices
- ❖ Privacy info
- ❖ Family Sharing & Game Centre support
- ❖ Available languages

Buy & download an application

- ❖ Touch the **Get** button or the price.

  If there's a Re-download icon ⬇ instead of a price or the **Get** button, it means you have already purchased the application, and you can get it for free now. Simply touch the Re-download icon ⬇ to download the application.
- ❖ If necessary, authenticate with Face ID or your passcode.

Give or share an application

- ❖ Click on the application to view its details.
- ❖ Click on the Share icon ⬆, then select one of the sharing options or touch the **Gift App** button.

Send or redeem an Apple Gift Card

❖ Touch the Account icon or your picture in the upper right part of the screen.
❖ Touch any of the below:
  ➢ Send Gift Card via E-mail
  ➢ Redeem Gift Code or Card

CAMERA

Learn how to take nice pictures with your iPhone's camera.

Launch the Camera app

Do any of the below to open the Camera:

❖ Click on the Camera app's icon  on the Home Screen.

❖ Swipe to the left on the Lock screen.

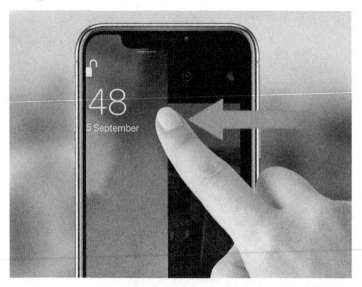

❖ Swipe down from the upper right edge of your display to reveal the Controls Centre, and then touch the Camera button

❖ Long-press the Camera button  on the Lock screen.

Note: For safety reasons, a green dot will appear in the upper right corner of your display when the Camera is being used

Capture a picture

❖ Enter the Camera app, and then touch the White shutter or press any of the volume buttons to snap a picture.

Move from one camera mode to another

The **Photos** mode is the default mode you see when you enter the Camera application. You can capture Live Photos & still pictures in Photo mode. Swipe to the right or left on the camera screen to pick any of the camera modes below:

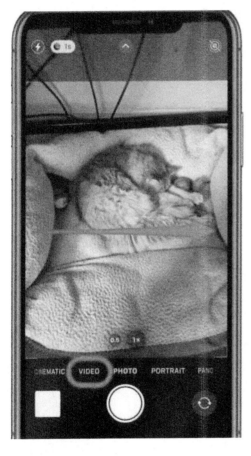

❖ Video
❖ Slo-mo: Record a slow motion video
❖ Portrait

- ❖ Pano
- ❖ Time-lapse
- ❖ Square
- ❖ Cinematic

Zoom out or in

Carry out any of the below to zoom in or out:

- ❖ Enter the Camera application and pinch open on your screen to zoom in or pinch closed to zoom out.
- ❖ Switch between 0.50x, 1.0x, 2.0x, 2.50x, 3.0x & 5.0x to zoom out or in. To get a more precise zoom, long-press the zoom control, and then slide the slider to the right or left.

Change the camera's exposure & focus

Before taking a picture, your device camera automatically determines the exposure & focus, and face detection balances the exposure of many faces. Adhere to the directives below to manually change the exposure & focus:

- ❖ Launch the Camera application.
- ❖ Touch the camera display to see the automatic exposure setting & focus area
- ❖ Touch where you want the focus to be

- ❖ Drag the Adjust Exposure button ☀ (beside the focus area) down or up to change the exposure level.

Tip: To manually lock your exposure & focus setting for future shots, long-press the focus area till the AE/AF lock appears; touch your display to unlock the settings.

To save the exposure control so it isn't reset when you close & open the Camera application, simply enter the Settings application, touch Camera, touch Preserve Setting, and then activate Exposure Adjustment.

Camera flashlight

The camera will automatically use the flashlight when necessary. Before taking a picture, do the following for manual control of the flashlight:

- ❖ Click the Flashlight button ⚡ to turn it on or off.

❖ Touch the Camera control button ⌃, then touch the Flash button ⚡ under the frame to select Off, On, or Auto.

Capture a picture with a filter

Use filters to add colour effects to your photos.

❖ Launch the Camera application, and then select Portrait or Photo mode.
❖ Click on the Camera Controls button ⌃, and then click the Filters button ⊛ .
❖ Swipe left or right to see filters under the viewer; touch one of them to use it.
❖ Touch the White Shutter to snap a picture with the filter you picked.

Use the timer

Set a timer to give yourself time to get in the shot.

❖ Enter the Camera application, click on the Camera Controls button ⌃

- ❖ Click on the Timers icon ⏱, and then select 10s or 3s
- ❖ Touch the Shutter to begin the timer.

Use Photographic Styles

You can use Photographic Styles which adjusts how the camera takes pictures. Select from the preset styles—Cool, Warm, Vibrant, or Rich Contrast—

and then adjust the warmth & tones value to personalize them. The Camera application will apply your settings every time it takes a picture in Photos mode. Adhere to the directives below to use a different Photographic Style:

- ❖ Launch the Camera application, and then click on the Camera Controls button ⌃ .
- ❖ Click on the Photos Style button ▱, and then swipe to the left to see different styles:
  - ➢ Rich Contrast.
  - ➢ Vibrant.
  - ➢ Warm.
  - ➢ Cool.

To personalize a Photos Style, touch the Warmth & Tone controls under the frame, and then slide the slider to the right or left to change the value.

Click on the Reset Picture Styles button ⟳ to reset the values.

- ❖ Click on the Photo Styles button ▱ to use the Photos Style.

To change or edit your preset Photos Style, click the Photo Style button  in the upper part of your display. To stop making use of a Photos Style, choose **Standard** from the Photos style options.

You can also change the Photos Style in the Setting application: Enter the Settings application, touch Camera, touch Photographic Styles, and then select one of them.

Capture Live Photos

A Live Photo captures what takes place before & after taking a picture.

❖ Enter the Camera application.
❖ Ensure the Camera is in Photos mode & that Live Photo is activated.
    When Live Photo is activated, you'll see the Live Photo icon in the upper part of the camera display. When there's a slash through the Live Photos icon it means that the Live Photo is off. Click on the button to activate or deactivate Live Photo.
❖ Touch the White Shutter to snap the Live Photo.
❖ To play the Live Picture, touch the picture thumbnail in the lower part of your display, and then long-press your screen to play it.

Take action photos with Burst mode

With Burst mode, you can capture moving subjects, or capture many high-speed images so that you have a range of pictures to select from. You can use the front & back cameras to snap burst pictures.

❖ Launch the Camera application on your device.
❖ Swipe the Shutter to the left

❖ Raise your finger to stop capturing pictures

❖ To choose the pictures you would like to keep, touch the Burst thumbnail, and then touch the Select button.

The gray dots under the thumbnails indicate the recommended pictures to keep on your device.

❖ Click the circle in the bottom-right edge of any picture you want to store as a separate picture, and then touch the Done button.

To delete the while set of Burst pictures, simply touch the thumbnail, and then touch the Trash icon

You can also hold down the Increase Volume button to capture Burst photos. Enter the Settings application, touch Camera, and then activate the **Use Volume Up for Burst** feature.

Tip: You can press and hold the up button to fire a burst. Go to Settings > Camera and use Volume Up for Burst.

Take a photo or record a video with your iPhone's front camera

❖ Enter the Camera application.

- ❖ Touch the Camera Selector button to switch to the front camera.
- ❖ Select Video, Portrait, or Photos mode.
- ❖ Place your phone in front of you.
  Tip: Touch the arrow inside the frame to enlarge the viewing area.
- ❖ Touch the shutter or press any of the volume buttons to snap a picture or record a video.

To snap a selfie that captures the shot as you see it on the front camera, instead of reversing it, Navigate to the Setting application, touch Camera, and then enable the **Mirror Front Camera** feature.

Capture panoramic pictures

Capture panoramic photos of your surroundings in Pano mode.

- ❖ Enter the Camera application.
- ❖ Select Pano mode.
- ❖ Touch the White Shutter
- ❖ Move slowly in the arrow's direction, while ensuring it's on the middle line.
- ❖ To finish, touch the Shutter once more.

Touch the arrow to pan in the other direction. Turn your phone to landscape orientation to pan vertically.

Capture macro videos & pictures

You can use your camera to capture amazingly clear close-up pictures & videos.

Capture macro videos or pictures

❖ Enter the Camera application, and then select Video or Photos mode

❖ Go near the subject—as close as 2cm. Your phone camera will automatically use the Ultra-Wide lens.

❖ Touch the Shutter to capture a picture or the Record button to record or stop recording a video.

Capture a macro slow motion video

❖ Enter the Camera application, and then select Slo-mo mode

- ❖ Touch 0.5x to use the Ultra Wide lens, and then go near the subject.
- ❖ Touch the Record button to record or stop recording the video.

Control automatic macro switching

You can control when your phone camera automatically makes use of the Ultra-Wide lens for snapping macro pictures & videos.

- ❖ Enter the Camera application, and then go near your subject
  When you enter the macro range of your subject, the Macro button 🌼 will appear on your display.
- ❖ Touch the Macro button 🌼 to deactivate automatic macro switching.
- ❖ Touch the Macro button 🌼 once more to reactivate automatic macro switching.

To deactivate automatic switching to the Ultra-Wide lens for macro videos & pictures, simply head over to the Setting application, click on Camera, and then disable Macro Control.

Capture photos in Portrait mode

Portrait mode applies depth-of-field effects to keep the subject sharp creating a blurred background.

Take a photo in portrait mode

❖ Enter the Camera application and then swipe to Portrait mode.

❖ If prompted, follow the instructions on your screen to put your subject in the yellow card box. Touch 1.0x, 2.0x, or 3.0x to switch from one zoom option to another.

Or, pinch open on your screen to zoom in and pinch closed to zoom out.

❖ Drag the Portrait Lighting control to select one of the lighting effects:

➢ Natural light.

- ➢ Studio Light.
- ➢ Contour Light.
- ➢ Stage Light
- ➢ Stage Light Mono
- ➢ High-Key Light Mono
- ❖ Touch the White Shutter to capture the picture.

After taking a picture in portrait mode, you can remove the portrait mode later. To do this, simply open a picture in the Photos application, click on the **Edit** button, and then click on the **Portrait** button to enable or disable the effect.

Capture a portrait in photos mode

You can apply the portrait effect in pictures captured in the Photos mode.

- ❖ Enter the Camera application.
  If your phone detects an individual, cat, or dog, the Depth button 𝑓 will automatically appear below the view finder.
  Note: Your device captures depth info when the Depth button 𝑓 appears while capturing pictures in Photos mode, so if you choose not to use the portrait effects, you can use it later in the Photos application.

Tap to turn portrait effects on and off in Photo mode.

❖ If you can't find the Depth button ƒ , touch the subject to make it the point of focus, and the Depth button ƒ will appear. Touch another subject on your screen to change the point of focus.

❖ Touch the Depth button ƒ , and then touch the White Shutter to snap the picture with the portrait effects.

Capture Night mode pictures

Night Mode allows your camera to snap more detail & brighten your photos in low-light conditions.

❖ Enter the Camera application. Night mode activates automatically in low-light environments.

❖ Touch the Night Mode button⊜ in the upper part of your display to activate or deactivate Night mode.

❖ To experiment with Night Mode, click on the Camera Controls icon⬣ , click the Night Mode button⊜ in the options bar at the lower part of your display, and move the slider to the right or left to select between Max & Auto timers. "Auto" sets the time automatically; Max makes use of the longest exposure time. Your selected settings are saved for the next night mode.

❖ Touch the White Shutter, and then set your phone to take the picture (make sure your phone is still)
Crosshairs will appear on your screen if your device detects motion while you're taking the photo - align the crosshairs to reduce motion & make the shot better.

Capture Apple ProRAW pictures

Apple ProRAW combines standard RAW format data with iPhone image processing to provide more creative control when you adjust white balance, colour & exposure.

Setup Apple ProRAW

Enter the Settings application, touch Camera, touch Formats, and then activate ProRAW & Resolution Control.

Capture images with Apple ProRAW

❖ Enter the Camera application, and then touch the ProRAW button or to activate ProRAW.
❖ Take pictures
While shooting, you can toggle between the Raw On or and Raw Off buttons to activate or deactivate ProRAW
To save your ProRAW settings, enter the Settings application, touch Camera, touch Preserve Settings, and then activate ProRAW & Resolution Control.

Change the default resolution & format of Apple ProRAW

You can set the ProRAW default resolution to 12MP, 48MP, or HEIF 48MP.

❖ Enter the Settings application, touch Camera, and then touch Formats.
❖ Activate ProRAW & Resolution Controls
❖ Touch Pro Default, and then select ProRAW Max, Pro RAW 12MP, or HEIF Max as the default format & resolution.

Change the shutter sound volume

❖ Enter the Camera application, and select Photos mode.
❖ Swipe down from the upper right edge of your display to reveal the Controls Centre, and then drag the volume button 🔊 down or up
❖ Swipe up to return to the Camera app

Record videos

❖ Launch the Camera application, and then swipe to Video mode.
❖ Click on the Record button or press one of the volume buttons to record the video. While recording, you can:
➤ Touch the White Shutter to snap a picture.

➤ Pinch open on your screen to zoom in & pinch closed to zoom out.
❖ Touch the Record button to stop recording the video.

Note: For safety reasons, you'll see a green dot in the upper part of your display when your Camera is being used.

Record 4k or HD videos

You can use your device to record videos in high-definition formats such as 4K (PAL), HD (PAL), 4K, & HD.

❖ Navigate to the Settings application, touch Camera, and then touch the **Record Video** button.
❖ Choose video formats & frame rates from the list.

Use Action Mode

Action mode provides better stability when you record in Video mode. Touch the Action Mode On button  at the upper part of your display to activate Action mode & the Action Mode Off button 🏃 to deactivate it.

Record ProRes videos

You can record & edit videos in ProRes, which provides better colour fidelity & less compression.

Setup ProRes

To setup ProRes, enter the Settings application, touch Camera, touch Formats, and then activate Apple ProRes.

Record a ProRes video

- ❖ Enter the Camera application, swipe to Video mode, and then click on the ProRes button ProRes HDR to activate ProRes.
- ❖ Click on the Record button to record the video.
- ❖ Touch the Record button to stop recording the video.
- ❖ Touch the ProRes button ProRes HDR to deactivate ProRes

Select the colour encoding option for your ProRes recordings

You can choose Log, SDR, HDR, colour encoding when recording videos in ProRes.

- ❖ Navigate to the Settings application, touch Camera, click on Formats, and then activate Apple ProRes.
- ❖ Touch ProRes Encoding, and then select one of the options.

Record a slow motion video

When recording in Slo-mo mode, the video is recorded as normal and you can only see the slow motion effect when you play it back. You can also choose when the Slow motion effect starts & stops in the video.

❖ Enter the Camera application, and then swipe to Slo-mo mode.

You can touch the Switch Camera icon to use the front-facing camera

❖ Click on the Record button or press one of the volume buttons to record the video. While recording, you can touch the White Shutter to snap a picture.

❖ Touch the Record button to stop recording the video.

To slow down part of the video and set the rest to normal speed, click on the video thumbnail and then click the **Edit** button. Drag the vertical bar at the bottom of the frame viewer to specify the part you want to be played in slow motion.

Record QuickTake video

A QuickTake video is a video recorded in Photos mode. While recording a Quick-Take video, you can put the Record button in the lock position & take still pictures.

❖ Launch the Camera application, make sure the camera is in Photos mode, then long-press the Shutter to record a QuickTake video.
❖ Slide the shutter button to the right & lift your finger when it's in Lock position for hands-free recording.

➢ You'll see the Shutter and Record buttons under the frame—click on the White Shutter to snap photos while recording

➢ Swipe up to zoom in on what you are recording, or if you are recording hands-free, simply pinch open on your display to zoom in
❖ Touch the Record button to stop recording the video.

Tip: Long-press a volume button to record a Quick-Take video in Photos mode.

Click on the thumbnail to check out the Quick-Take video in the Photos application.

Record videos in Cinematic mode

The Cinematic mode uses depth-of-field effects that keep the subject of the video sharp while creating a blurred background. Your iPhone automatically detects the subject of the video and keeps it in focus during recording; your iPhone will automatically move the focus point when it identifies a new subject. You can also manually change the focus point while recording or edit it later in the Photo application.

❖ Enter the Camera application, and swipe to Cinematic mode.
  ➤ To change the depth effect, click on the Adjust Depth button f and then drag the slider to the right or left before you start recording.
❖ Click on the Record button or press one of the volume buttons to record the video.
  ➤ The yellow frame on your display indicates the subject in focus; a gray box indicates a newly identified individual, but not in focus. Click on the gray frame to change the point of focus; touch the box one more time to lock the point of focus on that individual.
  ➤ If there's no individual in the video, touch anywhere on your display to set the point of focus.
  ➤ Long-press your display to lock the point of focus at a distance.
❖ Touch the Record button to stop recording the video.

Adjust the main camera lens

The default for the 1x Main lens is 24mm. You can add 28mm & 35mm as additional lenses, and choose a new default Main lens.

❖ Enter the Settings application, touch Camera, touch Formats, touch Photos Mode, and then touch 24MP.
❖ Enter the Settings application, touch Camera, and then touch Main Camera.

❖ In the Additional Lenses section, activate the lenses you would like to add as secondary Main lenses.

❖ In the Default Lens section, touch one of the options to use it as the default Main lens.

❖ Swipe up from the lower edge of your display to leave settings.

After setting up the main camera, open the Camera application. The Main camera default lens will be the one you chose in settings. Touch the Main camera lens to move to one of the additional lenses.

Change the resolution of the Main camera

The default resolution of the Main camera is 24MP. You can change it to 48MP, or 12MP.

Enter the Settings application, touch Camera, touch Format, touch Photos Mode, and then select one of the options.

View your pictures

❖ Enter the Camera application, and then touch the thumbnail on the lower left edge of your display.
❖ Swipe to the right or left to view your latest pictures.

- Touch your screen to hide or display the controls
- Touch the **All Photos** button to view all the videos & pictures stored in the Photos application.

Share your pictures

Touch the Share icon⬆ in a picture and then select one of the sharing options.

Use Live Text with your camera

Your iPhone camera can translate, lookup, share, & copy text displayed on the camera screen. The camera allows you to easily dial phone numbers, access sites, convert money, & more based on the text that appears in the frame.

- Enter the Camera application, and then set your device in a way that the text can be seen clearly on the screen.
- When you see a yellow frame around the found text, click on the Live Text button ⬚ and then carry out any of the below:

 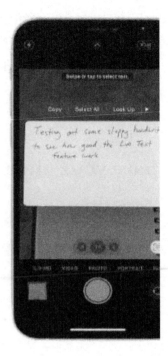

> Touch the **Copy** button to copy the text.
> Touch the **Select All** button to highlight all the text.
> Touch the **Lookup** button to display web suggestions
> Touch the **Translate** button to translate the text
> Touch the **Share** button to share the text with one of the sharing options.

Note: You can also long-press the text, then select the text you want with the grab points, and then carry out any of the actions above.

Touch one of the quick actions in the lower part of your display to do things like go to a webpage, begin an e-mail, make a call, etc.

❖ Click on the Live Text icon 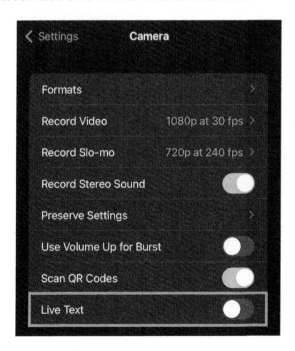 to go back to the Camera.

To deactivate Live Text on your iPhone's camera, enter the Settings application, touch Camera, and then deactivate the **Live Text** feature.

Use the camera to scan QR codes

You can use your phone camera to scan QR codes for tickets, applications, coupons, webpages, etc.

❖ Enter the Camera application, and then set your phone in a way that the code can be seen clearly on your screen.
❖ Touch the notification that pops-up on your display to enter the relevant site or application.

View videos & pictures in the Photos application

You will find all the videos & pictures on your device in the Photos application.

How videos & pictures are arranged on your device

You can navigate the Photos application using the Search, Albums, For You, & Library tabs in the lower part of your display.

Tap to navigate Photos.

View pictures in your library

To see your videos & pictures by when you captured them, touch the **Library** tab, and then choose any of the below:

- ❖ Years
- ❖ Months
- ❖ Days
- ❖ All Photos: See all your videos & pictures

View pictures in full-screen

Touch one of the photos to see it in full screen on your device.

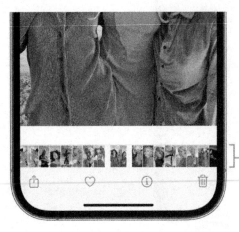

Swipe to browse through your photos.

Pinch open on your screen to zoom in on the picture and pinch closed to zoom out.

Click on the Favourite button ♡ to add the picture to your Favourites album.

Tip: When viewing a Live Photo ◎ in full screen, long-press the picture to play it.

Touch the Back button ‹ to continue browsing.

Touch the Delete icon 🗑 to delete the picture

View video & picture info

To view the metadata info stored in a video or picture, open the video or picture, and then click on the Details icon ⓘ.

Tap a circle to name someone identified in the photo.

PHONE & CONTACTS

To make a phone call in the Phone application, dial the number on the keypad, touch one of your recent calls or favourites, or pick any of the phone numbers in your contact list.

Dial a phone number

❖ In the Phone application, touch the **Keypad** button in the lower part of your screen.
❖ Carry out any of the below:
  ➢ Use another line: If you are using two SIMs on your device, touch the line in the upper part of your display, and then select one of the lines.
  ➢ Insert the phone number using the keypad, if there's an error, simply touch the Delete button ✕.
  ➢ Paste a copied number: Tap the number field at the top of the keypad, and then touch the **Paste** button.
  ➢ Insert a soft pause: Long-press the star (*) button till you see a comma in the field.

➢ Insert a hard pause: Long-press the pound button (#) till you see a semicolon on the field.

➢ Enter "+" for international calls: Long-press the "0" button till you see "+" on the field.

❖ Touch the Call key ◐ to make a phone call.

Click on the End Call button ◓ to end the phone call.

Call your favourites

❖ In the Phone application, touch the **Favourites** button in the lower part of your display, and then touch one of the contacts from the list.
❖ Carry out any of the below to manage your Favourites list.
  ➢ Add a contact to your favourites list: Touch the Add icon ✛, and then select one of your contacts.
  ➢ Delete or reorder favourites: Touch the **Edit** button

Redial recent calls

❖ Touch the **Recents** button in the lower part of your display, and then pick one of the numbers to call.

❖ Click on the More Details icon ⓘ· to get more information about the call and the person calling.

Call a contact in your contacts list

❖ Enter the Phone application, and touch the **Contacts** button.
❖ Touch one of the contacts, and then touch the number you would like to call.

Answer a call

If you have an incoming call, do any of the below:

❖ Touch the Answer button 📞

❖ Drag the slider if your device is locked

Silence a call

Press the side key or one of the volume keys.

Reject calls and send them to voicemail

Carry out any of the below:

❖ Double-press the side button.
❖ Click the Reject Call button .
❖ Swipe the call banner up

You can also slide the call banner down to display more options.

Carry out any of the below:

❖ Touch the **Remind Me** button, and then select when you would like to be reminded.
❖ Touch the **Message** button, and then select a default reply or touch the **Custom** button.

To create your own reply, enter the Settings application, touch Phone, touch Respond with Text, then touch one of the default messages and replace it with yours.

Change the sound while on a call

Press the volume button to change the volume level. Or swipe the banner down, and then carry out any of the below:

❖ Click on Mute to mute the call.
❖ Press & hold the Mute button to put the call on hold
❖ Talk hands-free: click on **Audio**, and then select one of the audio destinations

Start a conference call

You can setup a conference call with up to 5 participants.

❖ When you're on a call, click on the **Add Call** button, make another call, and then touch the **Merge Calls** button.
Repeat the process above to add more individuals to the call.

❖ Carry out any of the below while on a conference call:
  ➢ Talk to someone privately: Click on the More Info icon ⓘ, and then touch the **Private** button beside the individual. Click on the **Merge Calls** button to continue the conference call.
  ➢ Add callers on the same line: Touch **Hold Call + Answer**, and then click on the **Merge Calls** button.
  ➢ Drop someone: Click on the More Info icon ⓘ beside the person, and then touch the **End** button.

Assign a different ringtone to a contact

❖ Enter the Contacts application.
❖ Select one of the contacts, click on the **Edit** button, touch Ringtone, and then select one of the ringtones

Block unwanted callers

Carry out any of the below in the Phone application.

❖ Click on the **Recents**, or **Favourites** button. Click on the More Info icon ⓘ beside the contact or number you plan on blocking, scroll down, and then touch the **Block this Caller** button.
❖ Click on the **Contacts** icon, touch the contact you would like to block, scroll down, and then touch the **Block this Caller** button.

Manage your blocked contacts

❖ Enter the Settings application, touch Phone, and then touch Blocked Contacts.
❖ Click on the **Edit** button.

Create a contact

Enter the Contacts application, click on the Add icon ┿ , and then enter the contact details.

Find a contact

Enter the Contacts application, touch the search field in the upper part of the contacts list, and then type a number, name, or any other contact details.

Share contacts

Enter the Contacts application, touch one of the contacts, touch the **Share Contact** button, and then select one of the sharing options.

Delete a contact

❖ Enter the Contacts application, touch the contact, and then touch the **Edit** button.
❖ Scroll down and then click on the **Delete Contact** button.

Quickly reach a contact

In the Contacts app, touch a contact, and then touch one of the buttons under the name of the contact to start a message, make a call, etc.

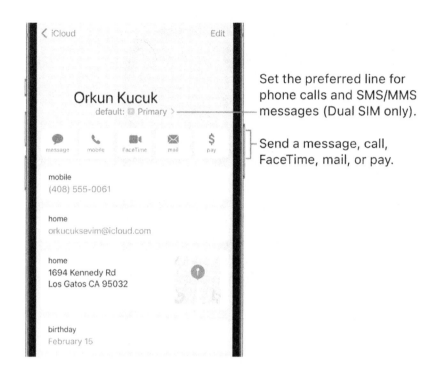

< iCloud   Edit

Orkun Kucuk
default: ☑ Primary >

Set the preferred line for
phone calls and SMS/MMS
messages (Dual SIM only).

message   mobile   FaceTime   mail   pay

Send a message, call,
FaceTime, mail, or pay.

mobile
(408) 555-0061

home
orkucuksevim@icloud.com

home
1694 Kennedy Rd
Los Gatos CA 95032

birthday
February 15

Edit contacts

In the Contacts application, you can assign a picture to one of your contacts, add a date of birth, change the label, etc.

❖ Touch one of the contacts in the Contacts application, and then touch the **Edit** button

❖ Enter or change their details
❖ When you are done, touch the **Done** button.

Add or edit your poster & picture

You can set a poster & picture to show automatically when you call or send messages to other people. To do this, simply follow the instructions below:

* ❖ Enter the Contacts application.
* ❖ Click on the **My Card** button at the upper part of your display, and then touch Contact Photos & Posters.
* ❖ (Optional) touch Name, then enter the name you want others to see, then touch the **Edit** button to choose a poster or create one.
* ❖ Scroll down and activate Name & Photo Sharing to start sharing your poster & picture with other people.

Use NameDrop to share your contact details with new people

The NameDrop feature allows you to easily share your contact details with nearby iPhones. Adhere to the directives below to use the NameDrop feature:

❖ Put the top of your device close to the top of another iPhone to share your contact details.
A light from the top of both devices lights up to indicate a connection. Keep holding & NameDrop will show on the two displays.

❖ You and the other person can now select any of the options below:
  ➢ **Share**: Receive the other person's contact details and share yours too
  ➢ **Receive Only**: Receive the other person's contact details.

To cancel the process, move both devices away from each other before Name-Drop completes.

Save a number you just dialed

❖ In the Phone application, touch the Keyboard button in the lower part of your display, type a number, and then click on the Add Number button.

❖ Click on the Create a New Contact or Add to an Existing Contacts option, and then choose one of the contacts.

Add recent callers to contacts

❖ Enter the Phone application, touch the Recents button in the lower part of your display, and then touch the More Info icon ⓘ beside the number.
❖ Click on the Create a New Contact or Add to an Existing Contacts option, and then choose one of the contacts.

FACETIME

Use the Face-Time application to connect face-to-face with loved ones—over WiFi or mobile connection.

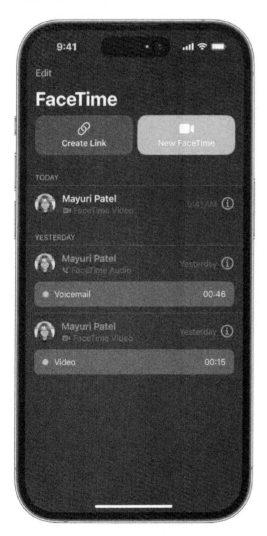

Setup FaceTime

Before you start using FaceTime, first enter the Settings application, touch FaceTime, and then activate **FaceTime**. In the "you can be reached by Face-Time at" section type your number or Apple ID if you have not already.

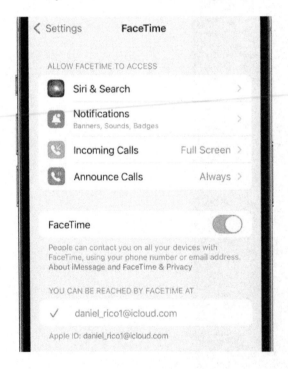

Make a FaceTime call

With an Apple ID & connection to the internet, you can make FaceTime calls.

❖ Enter the Face-Time application, and then touch the **New FaceTime** button.

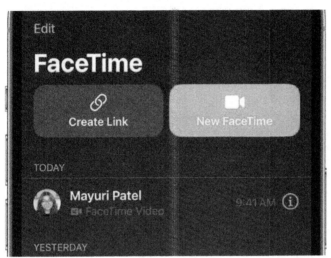

❖ Type the phone number or the name of the individual you plan on calling in the input field above, then click on the FaceTime Video button to make a video call or the FaceTime Audio Call button to make a voice call.

Or, touch the Add Contact button to enter the Contacts application and add a person from your contacts list; or touch one of the suggested contacts in your call history.

Record a video message

If the person you're trying to call does not answer your video call, you can record a video message and send it to the person.

❖ Click on the **Record Video** button, wait for about five seconds, and then start recording your video message.

❖ Touch the Send button to send the message, or touch the **Retake** button to record the message again. You can also touch the **Save** button to store the message in the Photos application.

After sending the message, the recipient will receive a notification.

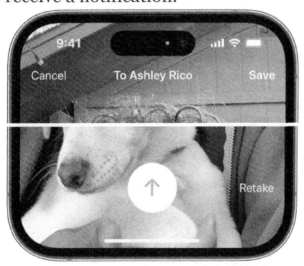

Receive FaceTime calls

When someone calls you via FaceTime, carry out any of the below:

❖ Touch the **Accept** button or drag the slider to answer the call.

❖ Touch the End Call key ⊗ or the **Decline** button to reject the call

- ❖ Touch the **Remind Me** button to set a reminder to call the person back
- ❖ Touch the **Message** button to send a text message to the person.

Receive video messages

If you missed a video call & the caller leaves a video message, you'll be sent a notification that you can tap to watch the video message. You'll also see a link to the video in your call history in the missed calls section.

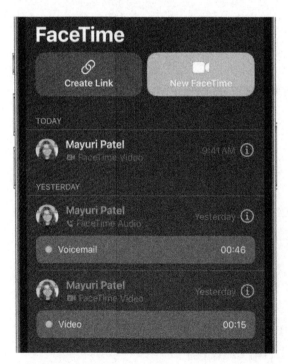

Delete calls from your call history

Enter the FaceTime application, swipe left on the call in your calls history, and then touch the **Delete** button.

Create a link to a Face-Time call

You can create a Face-Time call link & send it to other people, which they can use to participate in the Face-Time call.

❖ In the FaceTime application, touch the **Create Link** button close to the upper part of your display.

❖ Select one of the sharing options to send the link.

You can invite anybody to join a Face-Time call even those that don't have Apple devices. They can join the call from their browser, no login is needed.

Take Live Photos on Face-Time

When making a Face-Time video call, you can capture a Live Photo. Your iPhone camera captures everything that happens before & after you snap the picture, as well as the sound.

To capture Face-Time Live Photos, first, ensure FaceTime Live Photos is activated in the Settings application> FaceTime, and then carry out any of the below:

❖ In a call with another person: Click on the Shutter button ◯.
❖ In a group call: Tap the person's tile, click on the Full Screen icon ⤢, and then touch the Capture icon ◯.

The two of you will be notified that a picture was taken, and the Live Photo will be stored in the Photos application.

Activate Live Captions

While on a Face-Time video call, you can activate Live Captions to transcribe the conversation into text and display it in real time on your screen. If you have trouble hearing what others are saying in the call, Live Captions can make it very easy to follow.

❖ While on a Face-Time video call, touch your phone screen to see the Face-Time controls.

❖ Touch the Info icon ⓘ in the controls, activate Live Captions, and then touch the **Done** button. A Live Caption window will appear on your screen, displaying the transcribed dialogue of the call in the upper part of your display.

To deactivate Live Captions, touch your screen, touch the Info icon ⓘ in the Face-Time controls, and then deactivate the **Live Captions** feature.

Use other applications while on a Face-Time call

You can use other applications while on a Face-Time call.

Swipe up from the lower edge of your display to enter the Home Screen, and then touch an app's icon to launch the application.

To go back to the Face-Time screen, simply touch the green bar in the upper part of your display.

Make a group FaceTime call

In the Face-Time application, you can have about 32 participants in a group call.

❖ Enter the FaceTime application, and then click on the **New FaceTime** button on your display.
❖ Type the numbers or names of the individuals you want to call in the input field.

Or, touch the Add Contact button ⊕ to enter the Contacts application and add people from your contacts list.

❖ Click on the FaceTime Video button ⬛️🎥 to make a video call or the FaceTime Audio Call button 📞 to make a voice call.

Everyone participating in the call will appear in a tile on your display. When someone speaks or you touch a tile, that tile will become more prominent.

Add others to a call

Any participant can add someone to a Face-Time call.

❖ While on a Face-Time call, touch your screen to see the call controls, touch the More Info icon ⓘ in the controls, and then touch the **Add People** button.
❖ Type the person's number, Apple ID, or name in the input field.

You can also touch the Add Contacts icon ⊕ to add somebody from your contacts list.
❖ Touch the **Add People** button

Leave a Group Face-Time call

Touch the **Leave** button to exit the call.

Share your screen in a Face-Time call

You can share your screen in a Face-Time call to bring websites, applications, and more to the conversation.

- While on a Face-Time call, touch your screen to see the call controls, and then touch the Share Content icon .
- Click on the **Share My Screen** button to share the entire screen.
  A small image of your screen will appear in the call after three seconds. The other participants on the call can touch the image to make it bigger.

To stop sharing the screen, click the Stop Sharing Content icon .

Use video effects in video calls

❖ While making a FaceTime video call, swipe down from the upper right corner of your display to reveal the Controls Centre.

❖ Touch the **Video Effects** button, and then select any of the below:

➢ Portrait: This feature automatically places the focus on you while blurring the background.

Touch the More Controls icon to change the background blur level

- ➢ Studio Light: This feature dims the background & brightens your face. Touch the More Controls icon  to change studio light intensity.
- ➢ Gestures: This feature allows you to add reactions using hand gestures.

Add reactions in video calls

You can add reactions that fill your screen with basic hand gestures.

You can also add these reactions by long-pressing your tile and then touching the icons that pop up.

Note: To use hand gestures to add reactions, simply swipe down from the upper right corner of your display to reveal the Controls Centre, click on the **Video Effects** button, and ensure **Reactions** is activated. To show the reactions, simply perform any of the hand gestures below, and pause for a moment for the effect to activate.

Reaction	Gesture	Icon
Balloons		
Confetti		
Thumbs-down		
Laser burst		

Rain

Firework s

Hearts

Thumbs-up

Handoff FaceTime calls from your device to other Apple devices

You can start a Face-Time call on your phone and transfer it to another Apple device that you are signed in with the same Apple ID.

Note: Your selected contact info for the call, displayed in the Settings application> FaceTime must be the same as the selected contact info in the Settings application> FaceTime on the device you want to transfer the call to.

Handoff a Face-Time call from your device to a Mac or iPad

❖ While on a FaceTime call, carry out any of the below on the other device:
  ➤ Click on the notification displaying **"Move calls to this device"**.
  ➤ Click on the Video Handoff button ![Video Handoff button] in the upper part of your display.
❖ Adjust any of the settings, and then touch the **Join** or **Switch** button.
  The call will be transferred to the new device. On your iPhone, a banner will appear indicating that

the call has been transferred to another device; you can tap the Switch button in the banner to bring the call back to your iPhone.

Handoff a Face-Time call from your phone to Apple TV 4K

You can move a FaceTime call from your iPhone to your Apple TV 4K (second generation & after) when you are signed in with one Apple ID on the two devices. When you transfer the call, it will continue on your Apple TV. Your Apple TV will use your iPhone as its webcam & microphone during the duration of the call.

Switch to back camera

While on a Face-Time call, touch your tile, and then click on the Switch Camera icon 🔄.

Touch the icon 📷 once more to switch to the front-facing camera.

Turn off the camera

While on a Face-Time call, touch your display to see the call controls, and then touch the Video button ⬜◁. (Click on the button once more to turn the camera on)

Block unwanted FaceTime callers

❖ In your Face-Time call history, click on the Info icon ⓘ beside the e-mail address, number, or name of the person you would like to block.
❖ Scroll down, click on Block this Caller, and then click on the **Block Contact** button.

To unblock someone, touch the Info icon ⓘ beside the e-mail address, number, or name of the person in your call log, scroll, and then touch the **Unblock this Caller** button.

MAIL

In the Mail application, you can write, send, & schedule e-mails.

Change mailboxes or accounts.

Delete, move, or mark multiple messages.

Compose a message.

Filter messages.

Add email accounts

Before you can start sending & receiving emails through the Mail application, you must first add the e-mail account you want to use. The first time you enter the Mail application, you'll be asked to setup an e-mail account.

You can add more e-mail accounts to the Mail application from Settings. To do this, simply adhere to the directives below:

❖ Navigate to the Settings application, and touch Mail
❖ Touch Accounts, and then touch the **Add Account** button
❖ Touch one of the e-mail services—for instance, Gmail or Yahoo—and then fill in your e-mail account details.
 If the e-mail service you are using is not in the list, touch the **Other** button, touch the **Add Mail Account** button, and then fill in your e-mail account details.

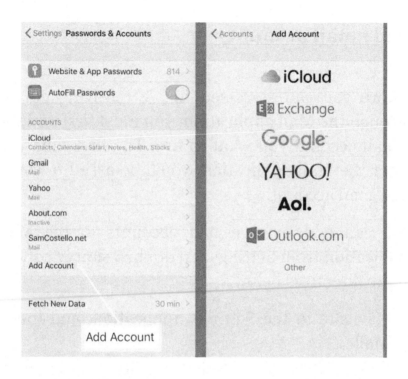

Temporarily stop making use of an e-mail account

You can turn off an e-mail account in the Settings application if you want to stop using it. You can easily turn it on anytime.

❖ Enter the Settings application, touch Mail, and then touch Accounts.
❖ Touch the e-mail account you would like to deactivate, and then carry out any of the below:

- ➤ Deactivate an iCloud e-mail account: Click on iCloud, touch iCloud Mail, and then deactivate **Use on this phone**.
- ➤ Disable other email accounts: Disable Mail.

Delete an e-mail account

You can remove an e-mail account from your phone.

- ❖ Enter the Settings application, touch Mail, and then touch Accounts.
- ❖ Touch the e-mail account you would like to delete from your device, and then touch Delete Account or Sign Out.

Read an e-mail

Enter the Mail application, and touch one of the emails in the inbox.

Use the Remind Me feature to come back to e-mails later

If there's no time to handle an e-mail at the moment, you can set a time to get a reminder and bring the message to the beginning of the inbox.

Click on the Reply button ↰ , click on the **Remind Me** button, and select the reminder time.

Preview an e-mail & more

If you want to see the content of an e-mail without completely opening the e-mail, you can preview it. In the inbox, long-press an e-mail to preview its content & view a list of options for muting, forwarding, etc.

Write an email message

❖ Enter the Mail application, and then touch the Edit icon ☑ .
❖ Tap in the e-mail, and then write what you want.
❖ To change the format, click on the Tools Extension button ‹ at the top of the keyboard, and then click the Text Format button Aa .

You can use a different font style & text colour, add numbered or bulleted lists, etc.

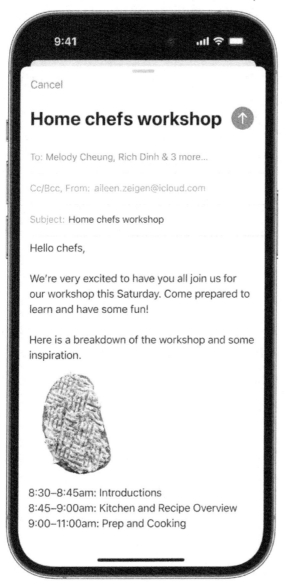

❖ Click on the Send icon to send the e-mail.

Add recipients

❖ Click on the To field, then write the recipients' names.

While typing, the Mail app will automatically suggest individuals from your Contact list.

Or, touch the Add Contact icon⊕ to enter the Contacts application and add people from your contacts list.

❖ If you would like to send a copy to others, touch the Cc/ Bcc field and then carry out any of the below:

➢ Click on the Cc box, and then type the names of the individuals you want to send a copy to.

➢ Touch the Bcc field, and then type the names of the individuals you do not want other recipients to see.

Schedule an email with the Send Later feature

Long-press the Send icon⬆, and then select when you want the e-mail to be sent.

Touch the **Send Later** button to view more options.

Send an e-mail from another account

If you have multiple e-mail accounts, you can choose the account you want to send an email from.

❖ In your e-mail draft, touch the Cc/ Bcc, From field.
❖ Touch the From Field, and then select one of your accounts.

Unsend an e-mail

You can change your mind and unsend an e-mail in the Mail application.

You have about ten seconds to change your mind after sending an e-mail.

Touch the **Undo Send** button in the lower part of the inbox to unsend the e-mail.

Delay sending e-mails

You can give yourself more than ten seconds to change your mind and unsend e-mails. To do this, simply enter the Settings application, touch Mail, touch Undo Send Delay, and then select one of the options.

Reply to an e-mail

❖ Tap in the e-mail, click on the Reply icon 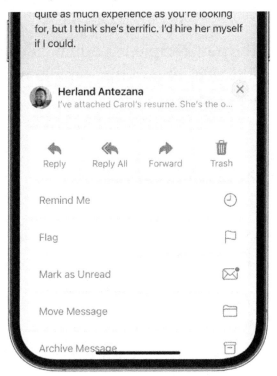, and then carry out any of the below:

- ➢ Reply to the sender: Click on the **Reply** button.
- ➢ Reply to the sender and other people: Click on the **Reply All** button.
- ❖ Type what you want.

Forward an e-mail

You can send emails to new recipients.

- ❖ Tap in the e-mail, click on the Reply icon ↰, and then touch the **Forward** button.
- ❖ Insert the new recipient's e-mail address
- ❖ Touch the text area in the e-mail, and then write your message.

Add email attachments

You can add documents, videos, & pictures to an e-mail for easy download & storage by recipients.

- ❖ Touch where you want to add the attachment in the e-mail, and then touch the Expand Tools button ‹ at the top of your keyboard.

❖ Carry out any of the below:

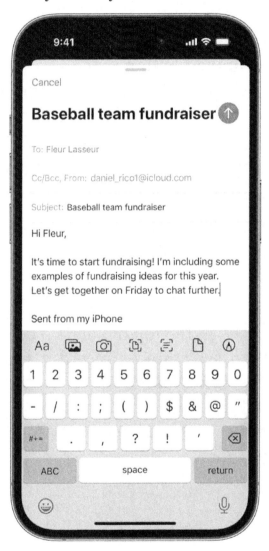

➢ Add a document: Touch the Insert Attachments icon at the top of your keyboard, then look for the file in the Files application.

In the Files application, click on the **Recents**, **Browse**, or **Shared** button in the lower part of your display, then touch a location, or one of the folders or files to open it.

➢ Add a saved video or picture: Click on the Insert Photos icon ⊞ at the top of the keyboard, and then choose one of the pictures or videos. Touch the Close icon ✕ to go back to the e-mail.

➢ Record a video or capture a picture & add it to the e-mail: Click on the Capture Picture or Video button 📷 at the top of your keyboard, and then snap a picture or record a video. Click on the **Use Video** or **Use Photo** button to add the file to your e-mail, or click on the **Retake** button if you want to take another shot.

Scan & add a document to an e-mail

You can scan a document and send it in PDF format.

❖ Touch where you want to add the scanned file in the e-mail, and then touch the Expand Tools button ‹ at the top of your keyboard.

❖ Click on the Scan Documents icon ⌞◻⌟ at the top of the keyboard.

❖ Set your device in a way that the page of the document can be seen clearly on your screen— your phone will automatically capture the page. To manually capture the document, click on the Shutter button ◯. Touch the Flashlight button ⚡ to turn the flashlight on or off.

❖ Click on the **Keep Scan** or the **Retake** button, scan more pages, and then click on the **Save** button when you are done.

❖ To edit the saved scanned, touch it, and then carry out any of the below:

  ➢ Click on the Crop icon ⌐ to crop the picture.

  ➢ Touch the Show Filters button ● to use one of the filters.

  ➢ Touch the Rotate button ◻ to rotate the file.

  ➢ Click on the Delete button 🗑 to delete the scanned file

Download email attachments sent to you

Press & hold the attachment, then touch the **Save to Files** or the **Save Image** button.

If you selected the **Save Image** button, you can view the file in the Photos application. If you selected the **Save to Files** button, you can find the file in the Files application.

Tip: To open the attachment with any other application, touch the **Share** button and then select one of the applications.

Annotate email attachment

In the Mail application, you can write & draw on a PDF attachment, picture, or video, then save it on your phone or send it back.

❖ Touch the attachment in the e-mail, and then touch the Mark-up icon 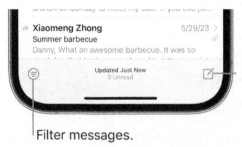.

❖ Select any of the drawing tools, and draw with your fingers.

❖ When you are done, click on **Done**, and then select one of the options on your screen.

Email filtering on iPhone

You can use filters to quickly display messages that match any criteria you select in the filter list. For instance, if you choose "Mail with Attachments Only", you'll only see your e-mails that have attachments.

❖ Click on the Filters button ⊜ in the mailbox list.

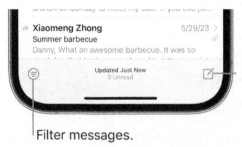

Filter messages.

❖ Click on the **"Filtered by"** button, and then choose or activate the criteria for the e-mails you want to see.

Click on the Filters icon 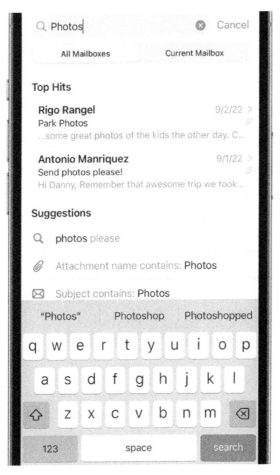 to disable all filters. To deactivate a certain filter, touch the **"Filtered by"** button, and then unselect it.

Search for an email in the Mail application

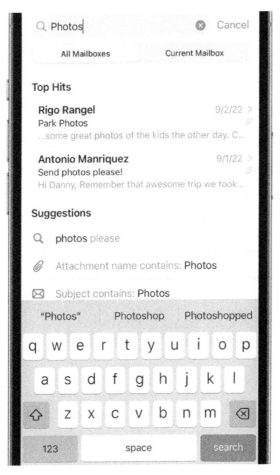

- In the mailbox, drag down to bring the search box out, touch it, and then write the text you want.
- Tap All Mailboxes or Current Mailbox.
- Click on the **Search** button, and then touch one of the emails in the list of results to open it.

Use Mail Privacy Protection

You can activate the Mail Privacy Protection feature to make it very difficult for senders to get information about your Mail activities. To protect your e-mail privacy, it hides your IP address from the sender, so that they cannot link it to your other online activities or pinpoint your location. It also stops e-mail senders from knowing if you have opened the e-mail they sent.

- Navigate to the Settings application, click on Mail, and then click on Privacy Protection.
- Enable Protect Mail activities.

Delete e-mails

There're different ways to delete e-mails. Carry out any of the below:

❖ Click on the Delete icon 🗑 while viewing an e-mail.
❖ While navigating through your e-mail list, swipe left on one of the emails, then touch **Trash**.
❖ Delete many e-mails at the same time: While surfing through your e-mail list, touch **Edit**, touch the e-mails you would like to delete, and then touch the **Trash** button.

Recover deleted emails

❖ Keep tapping the Back button ⟨ in the top left corner of your display till you see Mailboxes.

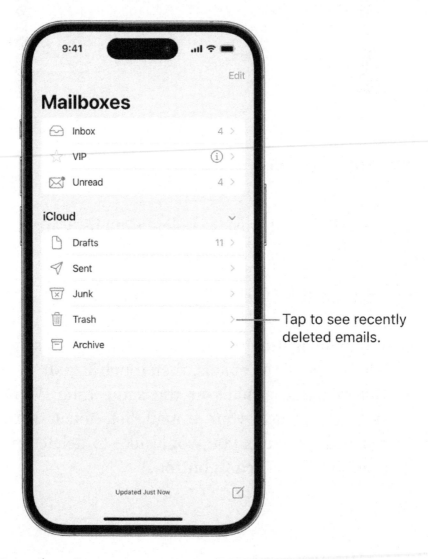

Tap to see recently deleted emails.

- ❖ Touch the **Trash** button ⌫, touch the e-mail you would like to recover, and then touch the Reply button ↰.
- ❖ Touch the **Move Message** button, and then pick another mailbox.

Print Email

In an e-mail, touch the Reply icon ↰, and then click on **Print**.

Print a photo or attachment

Click on an attachment to open it, click on the Share icon ⬆, and then touch the **Print** button.

MAPS

You can see your location on a map and zoom in to find the needed details in the Maps application.

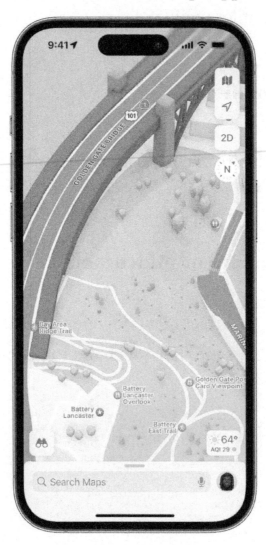

Allow the Maps application to use your location

To find your location & give correct directions, your device needs an internet connection via WiFi or cellular network and Precise Location has to be activated.

❖ If the Maps app shows a message stating that Location Services is deactivated: Click on the message, click Turn On in Setting, and then enable Location Services.
❖ If the Maps app shows a message that Precise Location is deactivated: Click on the message, click Turn On in Setting, click Location, and then activate Precise Location.

Show where you are on the map

Click on the Locate icon ◁ .

You'll see your current location in the center of the map. At the top of the map is the North. If you want the Maps application to show where you are heading at the top instead of north, touch the Headings button ◢ . Press the Directional Control button ⚓ or the Compass button ⊗ to start showing north.

Select the correct map

The icon in the upper-right part of a map indicates whether the map is for sightseeing 📖, satellite view 🌐, transport 🚋 or driving 🚗. Adhere to the directives below to use another type of map:

❖ Touch the icon in the upper right part of your display.
❖ Pick another type of map, and then click on the Clear icon ⊗ .

View a 3D map

Carry out any of the below on a 2D map:

❖ Swipe up with 2 fingers.
❖ Click on the 3D button in the upper right part of a Satellite map.

❖ In some cities, click on the 3D button in the upper right part of the map.

You can carry out any of the below on a 3D map:

❖ Zoom in to view buildings & other small features.
❖ Drag 2 of your fingers down or up to change the angle.
❖ Click on the 2D button to go back to a 2D map.

Move, zoom, or rotate a map or globe

❖ Drag the map to move around it.
❖ Zoom in or out: Pinch open on the map to zoom in on it. Pinch closed on the map to zoom out
❖ Rotate a map: Press & hold the map with 2 of your fingers, and then rotate your fingers.
❖ Explore the world with a 3D globe: Zoom out on the map continuously till it turns to a globe. Drag the map to move around it, or zoom in to find details for oceans, mountains, deserts, & more.

Download offline maps on your phone

You can save a location in the Maps application so that you can use it later when your device is not connected to the internet.

Change the size of
the map to download.

❖ Enter the Maps application.
❖ Touch your photo or initials beside the search box, and then touch **Offline Maps**.
❖ Touch the **Download New Map** button, and then type a location in the search box, or touch the **My Location** button.

❖ Select a region, and then click on the **Download** button.

Open or edit a map you have downloaded

❖ Enter the Maps application.
❖ Click on your initials or photo beside the search box, and then touch the **Offline Maps** button.

❖ Carry out any of the below:
  ➢ Touch the name of the map to open it.
  ➢ Change the name of the map: Swipe left on the map, and then click on the **Rename** button.

➢ Change the area covered by the map: Touch the name of the map, and then touch the **Resize** button on the map's image.

Change your settings for offline maps

If you have downloaded a map for offline use, you can change the settings such as when to download or update the map.

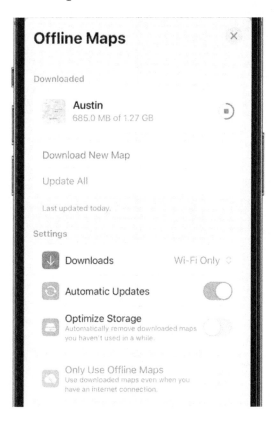

❖ Enter the Maps application.

❖ Click on your initials or photo beside the search box, and then touch the **Offline Maps** button.
❖ Scroll & select the settings you would like to update.

Find places on iPhone with Maps

Touch the search box, and then type a location.

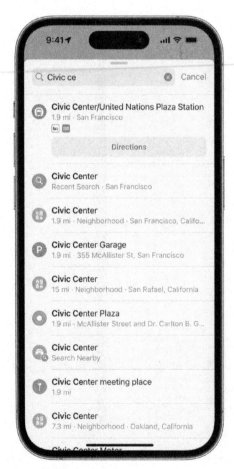

You can search in different ways. For instance:

* ❖ Crossroads ("9th & Market")
* ❖ Area ("Damascus Town")
* ❖ ZIP Code ("69329")
* ❖ Landmark (Statue of Liberty)
* ❖ Business (restaurants in London, movies, etc.)

Click on any of the results to get more details or receive directions to the place.

Find nearby attractions, restaurants, or services

Click on the search box, and then carry out any of the below:

* ❖ Touch one of the categories like Restaurant or Grocery Store in the **Find Nearby** segment of the card
* ❖ Type something like parks or playground in the search box, and then touch the "See Nearby" result.

Drag the map to change the surrounding area.

NOTES

In the Notes application, you can write down ideas or organize detailed information with check-lists, pictures, scanned docs, sketches, & more.

Create & format a new note

❖ Enter the Notes application, touch the New Note
  icon 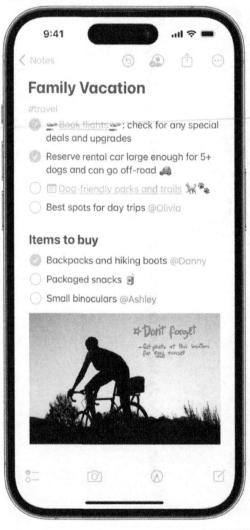, and then start typing in the text area.
  The 1st line of the note will become the name of
  the note.

❖ Touch the Format icon Aa to change the text format.
You can use a numbered or bulleted list, italic or bold font, etc.

❖ Touch the **Done** button to save the note.

Click on the Check list icon in the note to add a checklist, after that just type what you want, and tap on the **Return** button to move to the next item.

Adding or editing a table

In the note, click on the Table icon , and then carry out any of the below:

❖ Enter text: Touch one of the cells, and start typing. To enter text in another line in the same cell, simply long-press the Shift button and touch the **Next** button.

❖ Enter text in the next cell: Click on the **Next** button. When you get to the last cell, touch next to begin a new row.

❖ Format, add, delete, or move a column or row: Touch the 3 dots at the beginning of the row or above the column. Touch the 3 dots one more time, and then select one of the options.

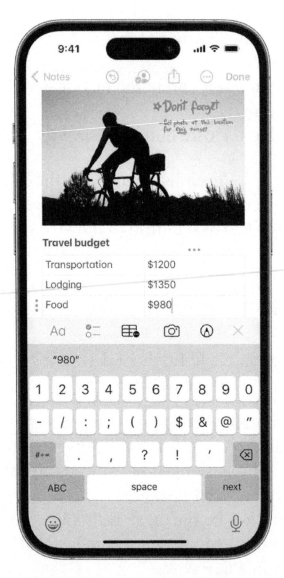

To delete a table and change its contents to text, touch one of the cells in the table, click the Convert Table to Text icon ⊞, and then click the **Convert to Text** button.

Draw or write in a note

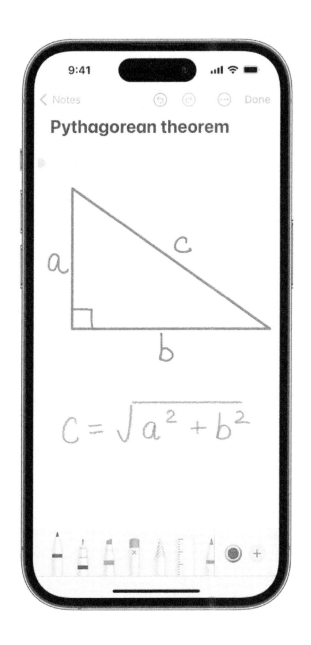

You can use your finger to draw or write in a note.

❖ Click on the Markup Tool button Ⓐ in a note, and then use one of your fingers to write or draw.
❖ Carry out any of the below:
  ➢ You can change the handwriting area by dragging the size handle (on the left) down or up.
  ➢ Change tools or colours: Use a Mark-up tool.

Select & edit handwriting & drawings

The Smart Selection feature allows you to select handwriting & drawings. You can delete, copy, or move the selection in the note.

❖ Click on the Lasso tool in the Tools palette.
❖ Highlight an object by circling it with the Lasso. Tool
❖ Touch the selection, and then select one of the options that appear on your display.

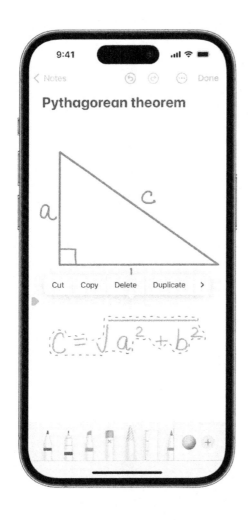

Scan text into a note using the camera

❖ Click on the Camera icon 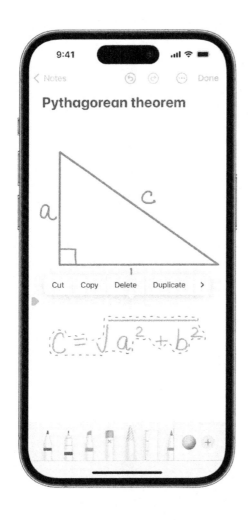 in a note, and then click on the **Scan Text** button.

❖ Set your device in a way that the text in the document can be seen clearly on your screen.

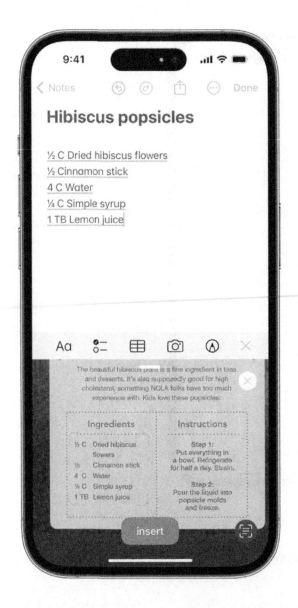

❖ Highlight the text you want using the grab points, and then click on the **Insert** button.

Scan the document

❖ Click on the Camera icon  in a note, and then click on the **Scan Document** button.

❖ Set your device in a way that the page of the document can be seen clearly on your screen—your phone will automatically capture the page.

To manually capture the document, click on the Shutter button ⬡ . Touch the Flashlight button ⚡ to turn the flashlight on or off.

❖ Scan more pages, and then click on the **Save** button when you are done.
The file will be stored in PDF format in the note.

Add a picture or video

❖ Touch the Camera icon ⬡ in a note.
❖ Pick one of the videos or photos from your Photos library, snap a new picture, or record a video.
❖ To change an attachment's preview size, long-press the attachment, and then select one of the options.

To store the videos & pictures captured in the Notes application in the Photo application, simply navigate to the Settings application, tap Notes, and then enable the **Save to Photos** feature.

Create Quick Notes anywhere on your phone

The Quick Notes feature allows you to easily write down thoughts over any application or screen on your phone.

All the Quick Notes you create will be stored in the Notes app.

Create a Quick Note

To start a Quick Note from any application, simply carry out any of the below:

❖ Touch the Share icon , and then touch the **New Quick Note** button
❖ Swipe down from the upper right corner of your display to open the Controls Centre, and then click on the Quick Notes button

(If you cannot find the Quick Notes button in the Controls Centre, you can add it – simply navigate to the Settings application, click on Controls Centre, and then select Quick Notes.)

View all your Quick Notes

To see all the Quick Notes you've saved, simply enter the Notes application, and touch Quick Note in the folders list.

Search for an item in a note

❖ Open the note

❖ Touch the More Options icon 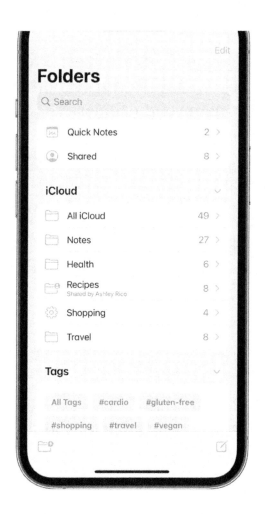, and then touch the **Find in Note** button
❖ Write what you are looking for in the search box

Create, rename, move, or delete folders

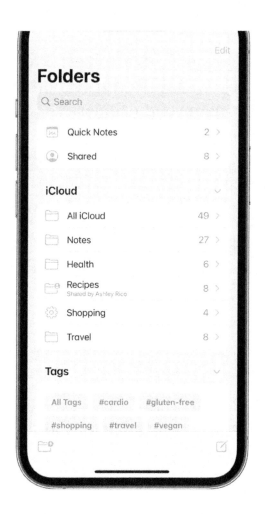

Do any of the below in the folders list:

❖ Create a folder: Touch the New Folder icon , pick one of your accounts (if you have multiple accounts), touch **New Folder**, and then give the folder a name.
❖ To create a subfolder, simply long-pressing a folder, and then drag the folder onto another folder.
❖ Change the name of a folder: Press & hold a folder, click on the **Rename** button, and then change the name of the folder.
❖ To move a folder, simply press & hold the folder, and then drag the folder to another location on your screen.
❖ Delete a folder: Swipe the folder to the left, and then touch the Trash icon . Or press & hold the folder, and then click on the **Delete** button

Pin notes

You can pin a note to the top of the notes list, to do this, simply long-press the note, and then touch the **Pin Note** button.

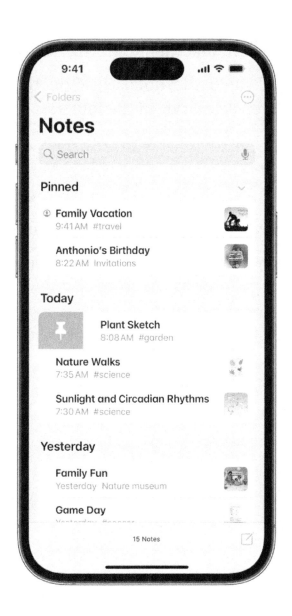

Move a note to another folder

Swipe the Note to the left, and then touch the Move icon 📁. Or, press & hold the note, click on the **Move** button, and then select one of the folders.

Delete a note

Swipe the Note to the left, and then touch the Trash icon 🗑. Or press & hold the note, and then click on the **Delete** button

BROWSE WITH SAFARI

You can surf the internet using Safari.

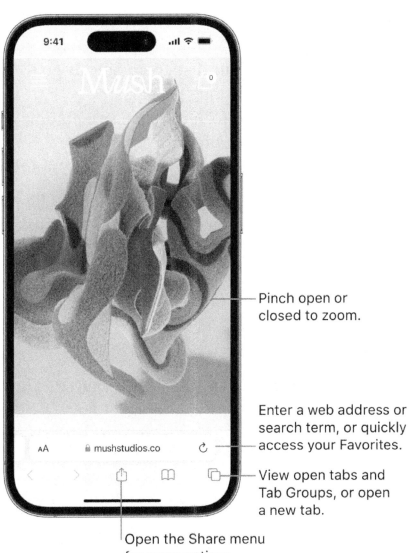

Pinch open or closed to zoom.

Enter a web address or search term, or quickly access your Favorites.

View open tabs and Tab Groups, or open a new tab.

Open the Share menu for more options.

View sites in the Safari app

Follow the guidelines below to surf through a webpage with ease.

❖ Return to the top of a long webpage: Double-tap the upper edge of your display to quickly go back to the beginning of a long page.
❖ Rotate your device to landscape orientation to view more of the website.
❖ Swipe down from the upper part of the **webpage** to refresh it.
❖ Share a link: Click on the Share icon on the webpage.

Preview a site link

Press & hold a link in a site to preview the link without having to open the page. Click on the preview to open the link, or touch the **Open** button.

Touch anywhere outside the preview to close the preview & remain on the current webpage.

Touch and hold a
link to see the URL
and these options.

Translate an image or webpage

When viewing an image or webpage that is in a language you do not understand, the Safari application can help you translate the text.

Click on the Page Settings icon AA , and then click on the Translate button .

Personalize the start page

The start page is the page you see anytime you open a new tab. You can personalize the start page with new options.

❖ Enter the Safari application
❖ Click on the Tabs button ⬜, and then click on the New Tab button ✛.
❖ Scroll down, and touch the **Edit** button at the bottom of the page.
❖ Pick the options you want to appear on the start page

Change the text size for a site

Follow the directives below to change the text size.

❖ Click on the Page Settings button AA in the search box
❖ Touch the small **A** to reduce the font size or the big **A** to make it larger

Change display controls

❖ Click on the Page Settings button AA, and then carry out any of the below:

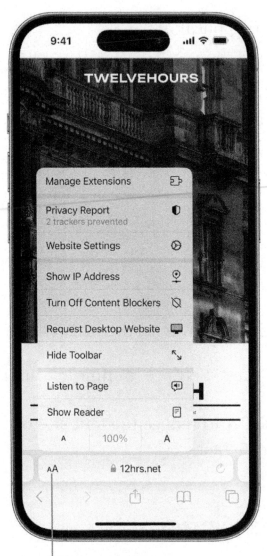

Tap to view the page in Reader.

- ➢ Hide the search box: Touch the **Hide Toolbar** button (touch the lower part of your display to bring it out).
- ➢ Touch the **Show Reader** button to see a streamlined view of the page.
  Click on the **Hide Reader** button to go back to the normal page view.
- ➢ Click on the **Desktop Website** button to see how the site looks on a computer.

Change other Safari settings

Navigate to the Settings app, click on Safari, and then change any options. For instance:

- ❖ Search Engine: Choose the search engine you would like to use when browsing in Safari (for example, Google, Bing, Yahoo, etc.).
- ❖ Privacy & Security
- ❖ Downloads: Select where you want the files you download from Safari to be saved
- ❖ Safari Suggestions: Decide if you want to allow Siri to recommend sites as you search

Change Safari layout on your phone

In Safari, you can choose a tab bar layout that suits your style.

Navigate to the Settings application, click on Safari, and then scroll to Tabs. Pick Single Tab or Tab Bar.

Browse web pages in Safari

❖ Enter the Safari application

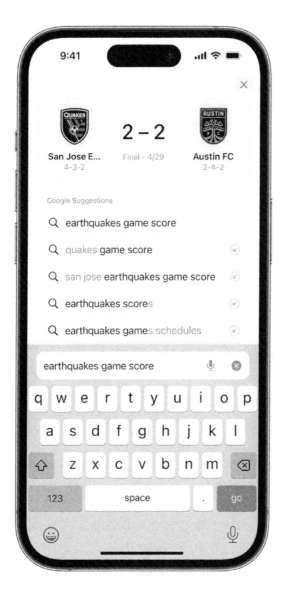

❖ Type a URL, sentence, or search term in the search bar.
❖ Touch one of the search recommendations, or click on the **Go** button on your onscreen keyboard.

Search for a term in a webpage

You can look for a phrase or word on a page.

❖ Touch the Share icon⬆, and then click on the **Find on Page** button.
❖ Type the phrase or word in the search box
❖ Click on the More Instance button ∨ to see other instances

Open a link in a new tab

In Safari, you can use tabs to navigate through multiple open pages.

To open a link in a new tab, simply press & hold the link, and then click on **Open in New Tab**.

To remain on the current page anytime you open a link in a new tab, simply navigate to the Settings application, click on Safari, click on Open Links, and then click **In Background**.

See the history of a tab

To view the pages you have visited in a tab, simply press & hold the Back button ⟨ or the Forward button ⟩ .

Close tabs

Touch the Tabs icon ⬒ , and then touch the Close icon ⊗ in the top right edge of a tab to close the tab.

Tip: To close all the tabs in a Tab Group at once, press & hold the **Done** button, and then click on **Close All Tabs**.

Open a recently closed tab

Touch the Tabs icon 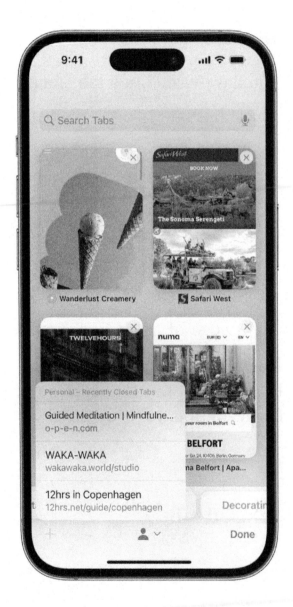, press & hold the New Tab button ✛, and select from the closed tabs list.

Organize your tabs

Create Tab Groups to organize your tabs so that you can easily find them later.

Create a new Tab Group

❖ Touch the Tabs icon ⧉ to see all your tabs.
❖ Press & hold one of the tabs, and then select **Move to Tab Group**
❖ Touch the **New Tab Group** button, type a name, and then touch the **Move** button.

Rearrange the tabs in a Tab Group

❖ Touch the Tabs icon ⧉ to see all the open tabs in the group.
❖ Press & hold one of the tabs in the group
❖ In the menu that pops up, click on the **Arrange Tabs By** button, then pick one of the options. Or, just drag the tab to the desired location.

Change the name of a Tab Group

❖ Touch the Tabs icon ⧉, and then touch the Group Tab icon ⌄.
❖ Click on the **Edit** button, and then click on the More Options icon ⊙.

❖ Click on the **Rename** button, type a new name, then click on **Save**

Move a tab to another Tab Group

❖ Press & hold the Tabs icon⬚, and then click on the **Move to Tab Group** button.
❖ Select any of the Tab Groups you've created or create another one.

Use Siri to listen to a webpage

You can use Siri to read some pages aloud.

Listen to a page

❖ Enter the Safari application.
❖ Go to the webpage you would like to listen to, and then carry out any of the below:
  ➢ Click the Site Settings icon AA, and then click the **Listen to Page** button.
  ➢ Summon Siri, then say "I want to listen to this webpage" or "Read this"

Pause listening

While listening to a page, touch the Listening Controls icon 🔊 , click on the **Listening Controls** button, and then click on the Pause icon ❚❚ .

To start listening again, touch the Listening Controls icon 🔊 , and then click on the Play icon ▶

Annotate & save a page in PDF format

In the Safari application, you can markup a page, write or draw on it, & share it with other people.

❖ Touch the Share icon ⬆

❖ Click on the Markup icon Ⓐ , and then use any of the available tools to markup the page.

❖ Click on the **Done** button, and then touch the **Save File To** button.

❖ Select a file to save it to, and then click on the **Save** button.

Block pops-up

Navigate to the Settings app, click on Safari, and then enable **Block Pop-ups**

Clear cache on your phone

You can clear your data & history to clear the cache on your device. This will remove the history of sites you've visited & searched recently on your device.

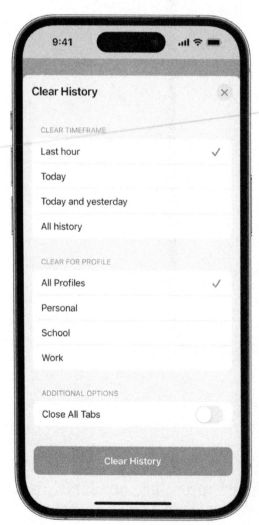

- ❖ Enter the Safari application, and click on the Bookmarks icon ▢.

- ❖ Touch the History icon ◔, and then click on the **Clear** button.

- ❖ Select the amount of data you want to erase

- ❖ Click on the **Clear History** button.

Visit websites privately

In the Private Browsing mode, you can visit sites in private tabs, which will not appear in your browsing history.

If your device has a passcode, Private Browsing will lock when you are not using it.

- ❖ Enter the Safari application

- ❖ Touch the Tabs icon ▢

- ❖ Swipe to the right on the tab bar in the lower part of your display till Private Browsing opens, and then touch the **Unlock** button.

To hide the website & leave private browsing mode, click the Tabs button ▢, and then swipe to the left to open a Tab Group from the menu in the lower part of your display. The Private mode websites will appear when next you make use of private browsing mode.

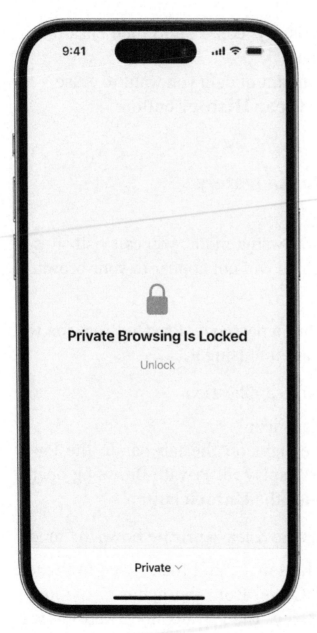

To deactivate Private Browsing locking, simply enter the Settings application, touch Safari, and then deactivate Require Face ID to Unlock Private Browsing.

Choose a search engine for Private Browsing

Enter the Settings application, touch Safari, touch Private Search Engine, and then select one of the options.

TRANSLATE

You can translate conversations, text, & audio from a different language to a language you understand in the Translate application.

Translate your voice or text

❖ Enter the Translate application.
❖ Click on the language you would like to translate the selected text to.

Touch the Swap icon ⇅ to swap languages.
❖ Click on one of the below:
  ➢ Translate text: Click on **Enter text**, type what you want to translate (or paste a copied text), and then touch the **Next** button on the keyboard.
  ➢ Translate your voice: Click on the Listen button 🎤, and then speak.
❖ When the translated text appears on your screen, carry out any of the below:

  ➢ Click on the Play icon ▶ to play the audio translation.

  Long-press the Play icon ▶ to change the playback speed rate
  ➢ Show someone the translation: Touch the Enter Full Screen icon ⤢.

  ➢ Touch the Copy icon 🗐 to copy the translation

Translate a conversation

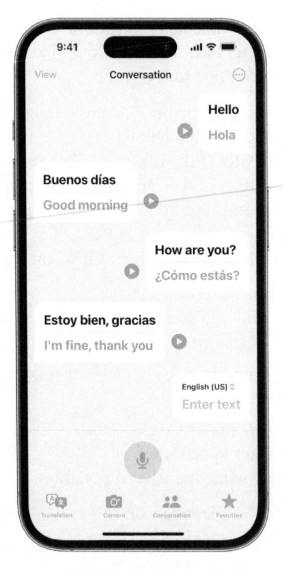

* Click on the **Conversation** tab
* Touch any of the below:

> Enter Text: Click on **Enter text,** type what you want to translate, and then click on the **Done** button
> Translate your voice: Click on the Listen

icon , and then speak.

❖ Click on the "Play" icon to listen to the translation.

You can set your phone to automatically play the audio translation, to do this, simply touch the More Options icon , and then touch the **Play Translations** button

You can translate a discussion without clicking on the MIC button before each person talks. Click on the More Options icon , click on the **Auto-Translate** button, and then click on the Listen icon to begin the discussion. Your device will automatically detect when you start & stop talking.

When having a face-to-face conversation, touch the **View** button in the upper left part of your display, and then touch the **Face to Face** button so that everyone can view the chat from their side.

Download languages for offline translation

❖ Navigate to the Settings application, and click on Translate.
❖ Carry out any of the below:
  ➢ Click on the **Downloaded Languages** button, and then click on the Download icon ⊙ beside the language you plan on downloading.
  ➢ Activate On-Device Mode

APPLE PAY

You can use Apple Pay to safely pay for items in stores, applications, & sites that support Apple Pay.

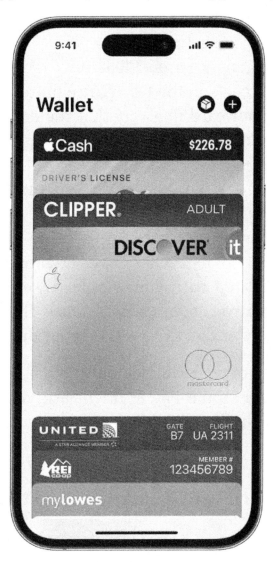

Add a debit or credit card

❖ Enter the Wallet application, and click on the Add icon ⊕ . You may be prompted to log in with your Apple ID.
❖ Do any of the below:
  ➤ Add a new card: Click on Credit or Debit Card, click on the **Continue** button, and then Set your card in a way that the details can be seen clearly on the screen, or insert the info manually.
  ➤ Add your old card: Click on the **Previous Cards** button, and then select a card that you've used before. These cards can include cards that you have removed, cards associated with your Apple ID, etc. Click on **Continue**, confirm with Face ID, and then adhere to the directives on your display.

Your card provider will decide whether your card is qualified for Apple Pay & might ask you for more info to finish the verification process.

View a card info & change its settings

❖ Enter the Wallet application, and then touch one of the cards.

❖ Click on the More Options icon⊙, and then touch one of the below:

> Card number.

> Card Details: Check out more info; change payment address; activate or deactivate transaction history; or remove the card from the Wallet application.

> Notifications: Activate or deactivate notifications

Find places that accept Apple Pay

You can use Apple Pay for secure, contactless payments in restaurants, stores, & more.

You can use Apple Pay anywhere you see the following payment logos:

Pay for items with the default card

❖ Press the side button two times quickly.
❖ When you see your default card, stare at your iPhone to confirm with Face ID or type your phone passcode.
❖ Put the top of your device close to the card reader and wait till you see Done & a confirmation icon on your display.

Pay with a different card

❖ Press the side button two times quickly.
❖ When you see your default card, tap it, and then select one of your other cards
❖ Stare at your phone to verify with Face ID or insert your phone passcode.
❖ Put the top of your device close to the card reader and wait till you see Done & a confirmation icon on your display.

Use Apple Pay in applications, Applications Clips, and Safari

You can use Apple Pay to make payments for items you purchase in applications, Application Clips, & online using Safari.

❖ When checking out, click on the **Apple Pay** button.
❖ Go through your payment details and set any of the below:
  ➤ Contact details
  ➤ Shipping & Billing Address
  ➤ Credit card

❖ Press the side button two times quickly, and then stare at your phone to confirm with Face ID or type your phone passcode.

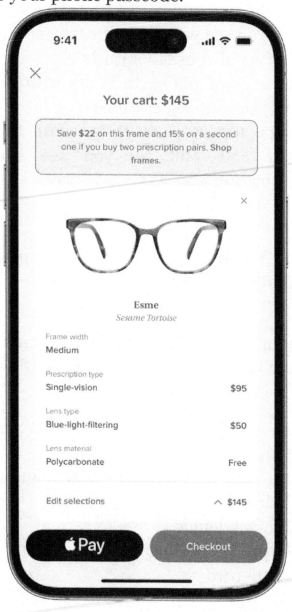

Change your information

❖ Navigate to the Settings application, and click on Wallet & Apple Pay.
❖ Set any of the below:
  ➢ E-mail
  ➢ Shipping address
  ➢ Phone

PASSCODE & FACE ID

Set a passcode

Set a passcode that has to be entered before your device can be unlocked when you switch it on or wake it.

Set or change your passcode

* ❖ Navigate to the Settings application, and then click on Face ID and Passcode.
* ❖ Click on the **Turn On Pass code** button or the **Change Pass-code** button.
  Click on **Passcode Options** to check out options for setting up a passcode.

Adjust when your phone automatically locks

Navigate to the Settings application, tap Display and Brightness, click on Auto Lock, and then select one of the available options.

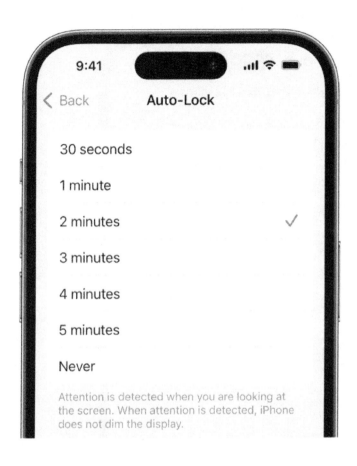

Erase your data after ten failed entries

Set your phone to delete all info & personal settings after ten consecutive failed password entries.

❖ Navigate to the Settings application, and then click on Face ID and Passcode.
❖ Scroll down and then enable Erase Data.

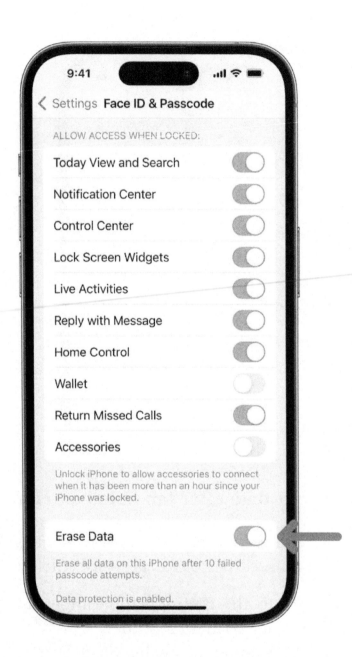

Disable the passcode

- ❖ Navigate to the Settings application, and then click on Face ID and Passcode.
- ❖ Click on **Turn Off Passcode**

Setup Face ID

With the **Face ID** feature, you can unlock your device, authenticate purchases & payments, and log in to a lot of 3rd-party applications by just staring at your phone screen.

Setup Face ID or add another appearance

- ❖ If you did not setup the **Face ID** feature when setting up your device, navigate to the Settings application, touch Face ID and Passcode, touch Setup Face ID, and then adhere to the directives on your screen.
- ❖ To add another appearance, navigate to the Settings application, touch Face ID and Passcode, click on Setup an Alternate Appearance, and then adhere to the directives on your screen.

Turn off Face ID

❖ Navigate to the Settings application, and touch Face ID & Pass-code.
❖ Carry out any of the below:
  ➢ Disable Face ID for certain things: disable any of the options.
  ➢ Deactivate Face ID: Click on the **Reset Face ID** button.

TURN ON/OFF, RESTART, UPDATE, BACKUP, RESTORE & RESET

Switch on your phone

Hold down the Side button till you see the Apple icon on your screen.

Switch off your phone

Carry out any of the below:

❖ Long-press the Side button & a Volume button till the sliders pop up, and then slide the Power-Off slider.

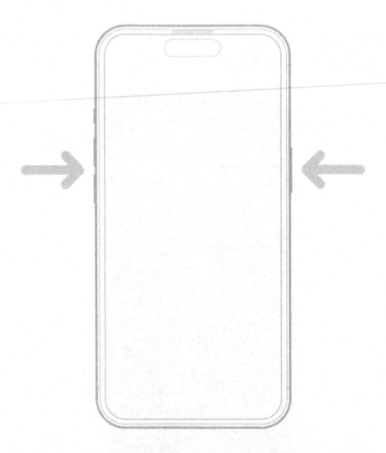

❖ Navigate to the Settings application, click on General, tap Shut Down, then slide the slider.

Force restart your phone

If your phone is unresponsive and you cannot switch it off, you can force it to restart.

- ❖ Press & release the Increase volume button.
- ❖ Press & release the Reduce volume button.
- ❖ Hold down the side button till you see the Apple icon on your screen.

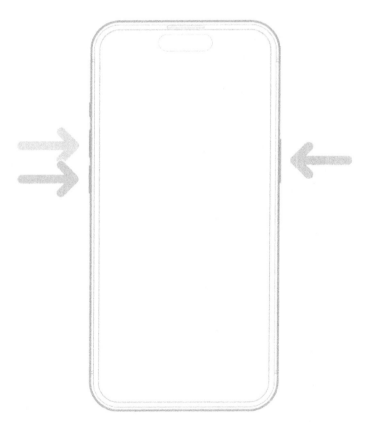

Update your iPhone's operating system

Before updating to the latest OS, ensure you backup your iPhone.

Update your phone automatically

❖ Launch the Settings application, tap General, click on Software Updates, and then click Automatic Update.
❖ Activate iOS Update in the Automatically Install & Automatically Download sections

Update your phone manually

❖ Navigate to the Settings application, click on General, and then click on Software Updates

Your screen will display the iOS version your phone is using at the moment and whether there's an update available.

Backup your iPhone

Backup your iPhone with your PC or iCloud.

Use iCloud to backup your phone

❖ Navigate to the Settings application, click on [your name], click on iCloud, and then click iCloud Backup.
❖ Activate iCloud Backup.
iCloud will automatically backup your device every day when it's locked, charging, and connected to WiFi.
❖ Click on the **Backup Now button** to back up your device manually.

To see all your backups, navigate to the Settings application, touch [your name], touch iCloud, touch Manage Accounts Storage, and then touch Backups. To remove a backup, select one of the backups from the list and then click on the **Turn Off & Delete from iCloud** button.

Use your Mac to Backup your iPhone

❖ Use your USB cable to connect your phone to your Mac computer.
❖ Choose your iPhone in your Mac's Finder sidebar.
❖ Click on the **General** button in the upper part of the Finder window.
❖ Choose **Backup all iPhone data to this Mac.**
❖ Select "Encrypt local back up" to encrypt & password-protect the backup.
❖ Click on **Backup Now**.

Use your Windows PC to Backup your iPhone

❖ Use your USB cable to connect your phone to your computer.

❖ In the iTune application on your computer, click on the iPhone button in the upper left part of the iTunes window.
❖ Click on the **Summary** button.
❖ Click on **Backup Now** in the Backups segment.
❖ To encrypt back up, choose "Encrypt backup", enter a passcode, and then click on **Set Password**.

Restore all content from a backup

Restore your phone from an iCloud backup

❖ Switch on your new or just erased phone.
❖ Click on Setup Manually, click on Restore from iCloud Back Up, and then adhere to the guidelines on your display.

Restore your phone from a computer backup

❖ Use a USB cable to connect your new or just erased phone to the computer that has your backup.
❖ Do any of the below:

- ➢ On a Mac(macOS 10.150 or after): Choose your iPhone in the Mac's Finder side bar, click on **Trust**, and then click on the **Restore from this Back up** button.
- ➢ On a Windows computer or a Mac (macOS 10.140 or before): Launch the iTunes application, click on the iPhone icon in the upper left part of the iTunes window, click on the **Summary** button, and then click on **Restore Back up**.
- ❖ Select one of the backups from the list, and then click on the **Continue** button.

If the backup is password-protected, you must insert your password before you can restore your settings & files.

Reset iPhone settings to defaults

You can return your device settings to their defaults without deleting your content.

- ❖ Navigate to the Settings application, click on General, click Transfer or Reset iPhone, and then click on Reset.

❖ Select any of the options:
  ➢ Reset all settings
  ➢ Reset the Home Screen Layout.
  ➢ Reset the keyboard dictionary.
  ➢ Reset location and privacy
  ➢ Reset Network Settings

Erase iPhone

Erase your phone to permanently delete your content & settings.

❖ Navigate to the Settings application, click on General, and then click Transfer or Reset iPhone
❖ Carry out any of the below:
  ➢ Prepare to move your contents to your new iPhone: Click on the **Get Started** button, and then adhere to the directives on your display. Once you're done, navigate to the Settings application, touch General, touch Transfer or Reset iPhone, and then click on the **Erase All Contents & Settings** button.
  ➢ Erase all data from your phone: Click on the **Erase All Contents & Settings** button.

USE YOUR IPHONE WITH OTHER DEVICES

Use your phone as a webcam

The Continuity Camera feature allows you to use your phone as a microphone or webcam for your Mac, thereby taking advantage of the powerful camera & video effects.

Note: Before you can make use of **Continuity Camera**, you have to ensure your Mac & phone are using the same Apple ID. Additionally, you need to activate WiFi & Bluetooth on both devices.

Select an external camera on your Mac

❖ Use a cable to connect the device to your Mac or connect it wirelessly.
❖ Enter an application that captures video, and then carry out any of the below:
  ➢ Photos booth: Click on the **Camera** button in the menus bar, then select your iPhone or a camera.
  ➢ QuickTime Player: Select File> New Movie Recording, hover over the window, click the down arrow ∨, and then select one of the cameras.
  ➢ Face-Time: Click on the **Video** button in the menus bar, and then select your iPhone or any other available option.
  ➢ 3rd-party applications: You can use your iPhone or external camera with 3rd-party applications. To learn how, just read the developer's manual.

Use your phone as a microphone or webcam

❖ Put your phone on a stand or place the back camera on the same side as your Mac's display. Your phone's screen should not be visible to you & make sure your phone is in landscape orientation.

❖ Enter an application on your Mac that captures video or has access to the Mic, such as Photos Booth or Face-Time.
❖ Follow the directives in the previous subheading to select your phone as the microphone or camera in the application's settings or menus bar.
❖ You can carry out any of the below:
  ➢ Pause the audio or video: Touch the **Pause** button on your iPhone. Or, unlock your iPhone.

- ➢ Resume the audio or video: Touch the **Resume** button on your phone. Or, press the side button to lock your phone.
- ➢ Stop making use of your phone as a Mic or webcam: Quit the application on your MacOS device.
- ➢ Remove your phone as one of the options: Touch the **Disconnect** button on your phone, and then confirm that you want to disconnect.

  To reconnect your phone, use a USB cable to connect it to your Mac.

Activate Video effects & Desk View

After using your phone as a webcam for your Mac, you can touch the Video icon in the menus bar and select any of the video conferencing features. For instance, Desk View displays a top-down view of your table, and Studio Light makes the background dimmer & brightens your face.

If you can't find your phone as a Mic or camera option

If you can't find your phone in the Mic or camera list in an application or Sound setting, try the following.

❖ Use a USB cable to connect your phone to your Mac & check once more.
❖ Check the following:
  ➤ You've activated Continuity Camera Webcam in the Setting app> General > AirPlay and Hand-off.
  ➤ Your phone accepts the Mac as a trusted computer.
  ➤ You've activated Bluetooth, WiFi, & 2-factor authentication on your Mac & iPhone
  ➤ Both devices are registered with the same Apple ID
  ➤ Both devices are within Bluetooth range (30ft)
  ➤ Your MacOS device is not sharing its internet connection & your phone is not sharing its mobile connection.
  ➤ The video application you are using has been updated to the latest version.

Handoff

The Handoff feature allows Apple device users to start something on one Apple device (iPhone, iPad, etc.) & continue from where they stopped on another Apple device. For instance, you can start replying to an e-mail on your phone & complete it in the Mail application on your MacBook Air. **Handoff** is compatible with many Apple applications, like Safari, Contacts, & Calendar & some 3rd-party applications.

Getting Started

Before you can use the Handoff feature, make sure of the below:

- ❖ Both devices are registered with the same Apple ID.
- ❖ You've enabled Hand-off, Bluetooth, & WiFi on your Mac, iPhone, or any other Apple device
- ❖ Both devices are within Bluetooth range (10m)

Handoff from another Apple device to your iPhone

❖ Swipe up from the lower edge of your display, and stop in the middle of your display to show the Apps Switcher on your phone. The Hand-off icon of the app you are making use of on your other Apple device will appear in the lower part of the Apps Switcher on your phone.

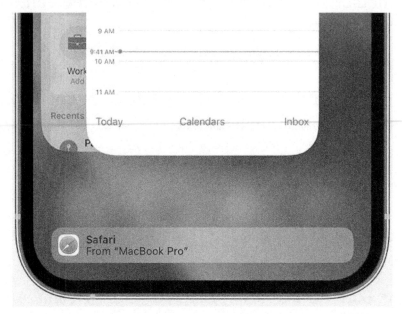

❖ Touch the Hand-off icon to continue working in the application on your phone.

Handoff from your phone to another Apple device

On other Apple devices, touch or click on the Handoff icon to continue using the application.

You can find the Handoff icons for applications you are using on your phone in the following places on your other Apple devices:

❖ iPad: on the Dock

❖ Mac: The right side of the Dock.

Activate or deactivate Handoff on your Apple devices

❖ IPhone, iPod touch, & iPad: Navigate to the Settings application, touch General, touch AirPlay & Handoff, and then activate or deactivate Handoff.

❖ MacOS 13.0: Select Apple menu 🍎 > Systems Setting, click on the **General** button in the sidebar, click on AirDrop & Handoff on the right of the window, and then activate or deactivate **Allow Handoff between this Mac & iCloud device**.

❖ MacOS 12.50 or before: Select Apple menu> Systems Preference, click on the **General** button, and then select or unselect **Allow Hand-off between this Mac & iCloud device**.

Universal Clipboard

Universal Clipboard, allows Apple device users to copy or cut content from one Apple device & paste it onto another Apple device. For instance, you can copy a picture or text on your phone & paste it on your MacBook Air & vice versa.

Getting Started

Before you can use the Universal Clipboard feature, make sure of the below:

❖ Both devices are registered with the same Apple ID.
❖ You've enabled Hand-off, Bluetooth, & Wifi on your Mac, iPhone, or any other Apple device
❖ Both devices are within Bluetooth range (10m)

Copy, cut, or paste

❖ Cut: Pinch closed with 3 of your fingers twice.
❖ Copy: Pinch closed with 3 of your fingers
❖ Paste: Pinch open with 3 of your fingers

You can also long-press a block of selected text, then click on **Copy**, **Cut**, or **Paste**.

INDEX

Printed in Great Britain
by Amazon